Declaring War Against Schooling

Personalizing Learning Now

Don Glines

ROWMAN & LITTLEFIELD EDUCATION
A division of
ROWMAN & LITTLEFIELD PUBLISHERS, INC.
Lanham • New York • Toronto • Plymouth, UK

Published by Rowman & Littlefield Education
A division of Rowman & Littlefield Publishers, Inc.
A wholly owned subsidiary of The Rowman & Littlefield Publishing Group, Inc.
4501 Forbes Boulevard, Suite 200, Lanham, Maryland 20706
www.rowmaneducation.com

Estover Road, Plymouth PL6 7PY, United Kingdom

British Library Cataloguing in Publication Information Available

Library of Congress Cataloging-in-Publication Data

Glines, Don E.
Declaring war against schooling : personalizing learning now / Don Glines.
p. cm.
Includes bibliographical references and index.
ISBN 978-1-61048-663-7 (cloth : alk. paper) — ISBN 978-1-61048-664-4 (pbk. : alk. paper) — ISBN 978-1-61048-665-1 (ebook)
1. Individualized instruction. 2. Student-centered learning. 3. School improvement programs. I. Title.
LB1031.G555 2012
371.39'4—dc23
2011040965

™
The paper used in this publication meets the minimum requirements of American National Standard for Information Sciences Permanence of Paper for Printed Library Materials, ANSI/NISO Z39.48-1992.

Printed in the United States of America

For Dr. J. Lloyd Trump, mentor, leader, educator, and visionary.

Now deceased, Dr. Trump served a variety of leadership positions, including principal at the pioneering Horace Mann High School in Gary, Indiana; professor, University of Illinois and coordinator of the breakthrough Staff Utilization Study; and his best-known role as associate director of the National Association of Secondary School Principals, where he conducted the nationally significant Trump Plan Model Schools Project. From approximately 1950 to 1980 he was recognized as the leader for innovation and change to improve the schools of America and meet the goals outlined by President Johnson. In his last book, he described how to create *A School for Everyone*.

Contents

Acknowledgments   vii

Prologue: Atlantic City   ix

1 Visionary Leadership   1

2 Educational War   11

3 Communicating Freedom   19

4 Startling Research   31

5 Looking Forward   51

6 Insightful Perceptions   63

7 Disturbing Priorities   77

8 Choice Alternatives   89

9 Exemplary Possibilities   105

10 Preferable Futures   121

11 Political Challenges   141

12 Successful Action   161

Epilogue: Personal Commitment   177

Bibliography   183

Index   189

Contents

About the Author   193

Acknowledgments

Visionary educators and politicians can cooperate in positive approaches for learning; there is no need for the current war against the negative one-size-fits-all policies of the Traditionalists. Recognition is due for the thousands over the 20th and 21st centuries who have tried to create personalized learning systems for everyone.

In the past five decades, the success of the renowned Wilson Campus School, Minnesota State University-Mankato, proved that humane cooperation is possible. Politicians approved, and educators implemented this unique year-round individualized option; Wilson illustrated that dream rhetoric is not theory, but reality. Very important is that the program was totally supported by state and local tax funds.

Cited for special recognition are representatives of the many Visionary Wilson/MSU faculty members who helped the author demonstrate that there can eventually be permanent Camelots:

Orville Jensen	JoAnn Lawson	Don Darling
Glenn Erikson	Margaret Schmidt	Lewis Holden
Gail Palmer	Perry Butler	Brendan McDonald
Don Sorenson	Tom Jeffrey	Gene Biewen

Dan Beebe	Michael Barkhurst	Karen Knight
Lynn Russ	Rosemary Doescher	James Nicholson
Larry Herke	Marvin Wolthius	Helen Holmes
June Bayless	Mark Schuck	Duane Orr
Cheryl Kalakian	Ann Courts	Kent Alm

. . . and researcher Dr. Kathleen Mary Long, University of Oregon, Eugene, who spent three years documenting every aspect of this story of Camelot.

Prologue

Atlantic City

Looking ahead during the early decades of the 21st century, it is yet important to glance in the rearview mirror. A disturbing reflection from a mid-20th-century meeting in Atlantic City asks a simple question: why fifty years later was this vision never achieved or even conjectured by Traditionalist politicians and school people?

Lyndon B. Johnson, a graduate of Southwest Texas State Teachers College, is often considered the most forward-looking occupant of the White House in recognizing the need to change from schooling to learning. An excerpt from his speech to ten thousand members of the American Association of School Administrators documents his dream for the future of education, though it was delivered long before the continuing explosion of technology.

Tomorrow's School

Tomorrow's school will be a school without walls—a school built of doors which open to the entire community. Tomorrow's school will reach out to the places that enrich the human spirit— to the museums, the theaters, the art galleries, to the parks and rivers and mountains. It will ally itself with the city, its busy streets and factories, its assembly lines and laboratories—so that the world of work does not seem an alien place for the student.

Tomorrow's school will be the center of community life, for grownups as well as children—a shopping center of human services. It might have a community health clinic or a public library, a theater, and recreation facilities. It will provide formal education for all citizens—and it will not close its doors any more at three o'clock. It will employ its buildings 'round the clock and its teachers 'round the year.

—President Lyndon Baines Johnson, Atlantic City, New Jersey, February 16, 1966

Chapter One

Visionary Leadership

Getting more learning out of our present schooling system would be like trying to get the Pony Express to beat the telegraph by breeding faster ponies.
—Edward Fiske

My grandmother wanted me to have an education so she kept me out of school.
—Margaret Mead

PRIORITY ISSUES

Should lawyers tell farmers how to plow fields? Should farmers tell doctors how to set broken legs? Should doctors tell merchants how to sell suits? Should merchants tell students how to study? Should all of these career people—as shortsighted politician legislators and school board members, most of whom know little regarding learning research—tell learners how to learn? The response to each is NO!

Traditional establishment persons should not be allowed to mandate unfair tests, unnecessary curriculum, and one-size-fits-all learning environments for all individuals or groups of learners. Visionary learning leaders know that warlike ACTION against the many issues of educational injustices is the immediate priority. The problem is not failing schools; rather it is failing *learning* systems directed by politicians.

School people know that low achievers have difficulty with traditional methods and curriculums. They will not admit that the structure of schooling also prevents most high achievers from maximizing their passions. Much of the blame for these conditions lies with the current submissive conventional educators who should refuse to accept the misguided solutions imposed by the rigid, controlling political bureaucrats.

It is not hard to understand why schooling is failing so many learners. There are numerous versions of the Animal School. This one is by George H. Reavis. It portrays most schooling in America today.

THE ANIMAL SCHOOL
Once upon a time, the animals decided they must do something heroic to meet the problems of "a new world." So they organized a school.

They adopted an activity curriculum consisting of running, climbing, swimming, and flying. To make it easier to administer the curriculum, all the animals took all the subjects.

The duck was excellent at swimming, in fact better than the instructor, but he made only passing grades in flying and was very poor in running. Since he was slow in running, he had to stay after school and also drop swimming to practice running. This was kept up until his webbed feet were badly worn, so he was then only average in swimming. But average was acceptable in school, so nobody worried about that except the duck.

The rabbit started at the top of the class in running, but had a nervous breakdown because of so much make-up work in swimming.

The squirrel was excellent in climbing until he developed frustration in the flying class where his teacher made him start from the ground up instead of from the treetop down. He also developed "Charlie horses" from overexertion and then received a C in climbing and a D in running.

The eagle was a problem child and was disciplined severely. In climbing class he beat all the others to the top of the tree but insisted on using his own way to get there.

At the end of the year, a monkey who could climb exceedingly well, but also run, swim, and fly a little had the highest average and was valedictorian.

The prairie dogs stayed out of school and fought the tax levy because the administration would not add digging and burrowing to the curriculum. They apprenticed their children to badgers and later joined the groundhogs and gophers to start a successful private school.

Does this fable have a moral?

The majority of learners, regardless of age, cannot excel in all the traditional curriculum areas, as illustrated by the animals. Even 4.0 grade point average (GPA) Yale graduates have weaknesses; they may do well in science, math, English, SAT tests, but may not do well in auto mechanics. Those with 2.0 GPA standings, or lower, often have tremendous strengths, if allowed to pursue their talents. In politics, Harry Truman was considered initially by many to be a "buffoon." He emerged as one of the most outstanding U.S. presidents.

PERSONALIZED SOLUTIONS

There is a simple solution to such problems. In education, the focus should be to build first on the strengths and interests of the individual, not on the weaknesses and failures of those considered low achievers. The no-cost response is the concept of personalized learning or personalizing learning systems. Personalizing does not reflect one teacher preparing individual lessons all day for every student, whether 30 in a self-contained classroom, 150 in five classes of 30 in a period 1-2-3 configuration, or a college lecture hall of 300.

Instead, personalizing is a learner-managed learning system, almost birth to death, but certainly in conventional K–12 and college levels. Students plan and manage their own daily activities (yes, kindergarteners, too) with assistance from their self-selected advisors. They learn on their own, or in groups of four to twelve, or any desired size. When needing assistance, they ask other students who know the next steps, or seek direction from a professional "guide-by-the-side," not a "sage-on-the-stage."

Is such a change essential to maximize learning for almost 100 percent of the students—whether A or F learners? Yes! U.S. Department of Education statistics published in 2011 indicate that perhaps seven thousand K–12 youth, called dropouts, are being "pushed out" of schooling every day. Of those remaining in traditional mandated routines, 30 percent have D/F report cards and GPA levels; 40 percent "excited" learners receive a C report card. Thus, 70 percent of the students in the awful current schooling system are at best unsatisfactory, mediocre, or failing. This does not reflect a learning system.

The A/B "going to college" youth are bored with their overall schooling—even if they receive a scholarship or enjoy being on the basketball team, the student council, or attending social events. Advanced Placement classes, more hours, and unnecessary "homework" may help with a scholarship, but not with an "I love learning" feeling. As the Animal School shows, erroneous traditional schooling curriculum patterns have been obvious for decades, but the Traditional Army has not retreated.

For example, learning leaders know that foreign languages should be learned through concentrated immersion programs in K–4, at home, or in preschool. But schooling has created a formula for illiteracy at the secondary level: 55 times 5 times 9 times 2! Few, if any, can study French (or another language) fifty-five minutes a day, five days a week, nine months a year, times two. Yet, though students fail to graduate with any language competency, these two years meet most university entrance requirements.

MULTIPLE OPTIONS

The Traditionalist Army states that it is impossible to change the system. Students must have science and math. Futurist Robert Theobald met their objections with a very simple statement: "It is time to do the impossible: the possible is no longer working." For the near term, school buildings will continue in spite of the availability of online learning.

The labor unions will not want youth competing for jobs, the police do not want youth on the streets five additional days, the colleges are already overcrowded, and most parents will want a safe haven for their offspring while they are at work. But the impossible can become possible.

At no additional cost, by offering all families alternatives, options can be provided. A simple schools-within-a-school structure illustrates that districts can, as one of many possibilities, provide a choice of (a) traditional, (b) modified flexible, or (c) personalized learning programs within one building.

Can options really work? Yes, even many "gifted" students are dropping out of schooling. The grandson of the author skipped grades ten, eleven, and twelve, entered community college for two years, and then two years later graduated from the famed University of California at Berkeley without attending high school or receiving a high school diploma. The process is simple for those who select this route.

It is obvious to the Visionary Army that one-size-fits-all school-ing, which traps almost 100 percent of the learners, makes no edu-cational sense. If a valid statement, why have neither the Visionar-ies nor the Traditionalists overcome this "tragedy of education"?

ENEMY CONTROL

Why have Visionary advocates of "learning" not been able to de-feat Traditional defenders of "schooling"? The immediate response is the stranglehold control held by Traditionalist politicians, includ-ing school boards. No Child Left Behind (NCLB) was the wrong approach and poorly implemented. Race to the Top was even worse, as were the policies proposed by Secretary of Education Arne Duncan.

Further failures have been caused by educators who have re-fused to say NO to bad legislation. Requiring algebra to graduate, and requiring reading in kindergarten for ALL are wrong, but teacher unions and education organizations bowed to the wind of politics. The traditional American seventh grade, discussed later, is the worst calamity in the education world; yet it still exists.

As Linus said to Charlie Brown: "I guess it is wrong always to worry about tomorrow—maybe we should only worry about to-day." Charlie Brown replied: "Nope, that's giving up. I'm still hoping yesterday will get better." Traditionalists are still hoping that yesterday will get better—by such means as Race to the Top. Visionaries realize that only if significant changes are made—schooling to learning—will there be a chance for a better educa-tional tomorrow. They believe that one-size-fits-all uniformity is not democracy.

Politicians claim they have tried to improve education by intro-ducing changes such as NCLB, vouchers, and charters. However, these are all accomplished through mandated traditional curriculum and continuation of A-B-C report cards, more tests, more homework, "world-class standards," and self-contained teacher-dominated classrooms. Charters could have been great, but school boards ruined the concept by imposing strict approval policies.

The "Governor's Schools" programs in a number of states were only for a few, and most were later closed. Mastery and differentiated learning styles were never fully understood and were utilized by only a few districts. The theories may have been positive, but where implemented never made a significant difference for learners.

VISIONARY FAILURES

During the President Johnson era and well into the 1970s, Visionaries were able to create exciting programs. The Model Schools Project involving twenty selected sites, supported by the National Association of Secondary School Principals (NASSP) and by Danforth Foundation funding, had the highest expectations, but the project eventually failed. Traditionalists gained control of school boards; the "leaders" who initially approved participation as a national "model school" accepted positions elsewhere.

Visionaries often became their own victims. They launched exciting new programs, were on the national visitation list, and were asked to conduct workshops. They became so entrenched, believing that they had invented Nirvana, that they refused to retool and create ongoing renewal. Often the leaders left, or the local cultural composition changed. The pioneering school became stagnant.

However, in almost all of the previously innovative programs that failed, the problems were again twofold:

1. Traditionalist politicians passed misguided education requirements; at the local level, elections led to win/lose school boards hiring conventional superintendents, who then eliminated most of the diverse programs.

2. Visionaries failed to fight hard enough. They succumbed to the smart politicians who claimed the change agents were too radical, living in the past, were too far ahead of the times, were wild idealists with no documented proof, joiners of new fads, or the usual favorite—out of touch with reality.

The Traditionalists also claimed Visionaries were against accountability. The politicians wanted an easy platform stating that all students had an equal chance for college; they rejected the notion that the billions spent on testing were unjustified. The students, advisors, and parents knew what they knew without "standardized tests." If proof were needed as to whether the learner passed taxidermy, just ask him or her to "stuff the bird." Students are honest without tests and "grades" for evaluation.

UNDERSTANDING GOALS

The goal of *Declaring War Against Schooling* is to create a national movement by schooling and societal critics to overthrow the controlling political Traditionalists. It is a plea for ACTION! This must be a GROUP effort of individual Visionaries willing to stand tall and demand relief from the current illogical system imposed by rigid conventional voters. The Visionaries must explain how choices can be provided, and why it is necessary to create significantly different and better learning—not schooling—systems for now and the longer-term future.

Powerful ACTION STEPS really can be achieved, leading to solutions of differences between the warring armies. A win/win rather than the longstanding win/lose philosophy is the beginning of the transformation toward freedom and choice for learners of all ages. For now, continuance of the famous 100 YEARS WAR is essential in seeking new directions. However, the path to the future has been mapped by two precious Epcot Center guides. Figment and his friend Dreamfinder illustrate how, through a journey of IMAGINEERING—imagining, inventing, and implementing.

Chapter Two

Educational War

Schools have not much to do with education; they are mainly institutions of control where certain basic habits must be instilled in the young. Education is quite different and has little place in school.
—Winston Churchill

DECLARING WAR

The emerging leaders of the Visionary Army of societal and learning critics—joined by veterans of decades of battles against unvalidated traditions—have declared a renewed effort in the continuing war against the enemy: the hordes of self-proclaimed saviors of schooling—the Traditionalist Army. This militant command has maintained its conquest of "education" by reinforcing and reinventing long tolerated systems of oppressive "schooling."

The Traditionalist Army has been supported by moneyed individuals and power groups who benefit from requiring schooling atrocities. They know only what they themselves managed to endure; they do not understand the concept of options or multiple learning systems—birth to death—for everyone. This especially applies to the obsolete K–12 and four-year college structures.

Politicians have usurped the roles of those learning Visionaries who prepared to lead. Teachers unions have not been learning leaders; they fight to protect wages, hours, and benefits, but never strike for students. Other than limited health, safety, and budget issues, politicians and unions should have no role in establishing the best learning opportunities for each learner.

JUSTIFIED ANALOGIES

The 100 Years War (1337 to 1453—116 years) has been cited as the longest in history. However, that conflict pales when contrasted with the centuries old on/off WAR AGAINST LEARNING. The battles continue between (1) *Traditionalist* politicians and school people who favor "reforming schooling," and (2) *Visionary* societal and educational critics who advocate "personalized learning environments."

These latter voices profess that one-size-fits-all schooling and testing does not benefit the great majority. The goal is to eradicate required edicts in favor of learner, mentor, and family-directed formats through options and choices. Research studies and experimental projects have overwhelmingly supported personalization. Why then are 95 percent of the mandated learners in America still subjected to Traditionalist Army imposed controls?

The analogies in education to a shooting war reflect the same mentality. Wartime struggles exist between the conquering Traditionalists and the suppressed Visionaries. How often must voters be reminded that traditional schooling (Germany had one of the best systems) produced not only V-2 rockets but also concentration camps such as Auschwitz, Treblinka, Dachau, and Buchenwald, as well as numerous labor and transit camps—twenty thousand (yes!) where millions were worked to death and slaughtered.

Vivien Spitz's book *Doctors from Hell* portrays the unbelievably brutal experiments on humans performed by *brilliant* and *highly educated* German physicians. Though Poland was almost destroyed by these same "well-schooled" Germans, the amazing resistance of the Polish people provided an inspirational example of courage against an aggressor.

Courage was displayed at Iwo Jima and Okinawa against another "well-schooled," highly educated nation. It is hard to forgive the Japanese for their ugly brutalities, not only against Americans after Pearl Harbor, but for such acts as the 1937 "Rape of Nanking" where ninety thousand surrendering Chinese soldiers were massacred. Persons who claim to be educators must muster the strength of the crews of the unreliable B-24 bombers; they flew missions early in the World War II Pacific theater, knowing of their slim chance of returning.

For the sake of future generations, it is time for enough bravery to refuse to accept bad learning decisions made by POLITICIANS. History abounds with thousands of courageous realities through many wars. Visionary learning leaders need fortitude. Two recent books, *The Zookeeper's Wife* and *Unbroken*, document the German-, and especially the cruel Japanese-inflicted human tragedies. However, these two countries had high "test scores."

PHYSICAL ACTION

Action by the current Visionary Army must become more forceful! Direct, personal face-to-face confrontations—verbal, immediate, uncompromising combat by the forces opposing the Traditionalist Army cannot wait beyond NOW! Attacks must increase against the United States Congress, the national Department of Education, state legislatures, local school boards (they are only politicians), and Traditionalist one-view schooling administrators with uncompromising demands.

The concepts of the 1966 speech by President Johnson (see the prologue) were being implemented in the 1970s by the Visionaries but were halted in the 1980s. Three decades later, it is wrong to remain silent. Attacks by books and articles have only kept the hope for tomorrow alive, but these efforts have failed to dislodge the enemy.

The response from the controlling conquerors to "failing students and schools" has been to fire more teachers and administrators, close more buildings, mandate additional "academic" time and curriculum, and force harder tests of loyalty to their cause. Eliminating tenure, adopting merit pay, and similar actions are all in the wrong direction and will not help learning.

The justification for such backward Traditionalist punishment has been the propaganda of addressing poverty to reduce the gap in math and reading scores between—in general—the higher-achieving Caucasian and Asian, and the lower-achieving Hispanic, African-American, and Native American students. People of diverse cultures are exceptional in fields such as art, music, physical education, and languages. It is wonderful to be bilingual. Why are math and science scores the benchmark for talent?

The majority of learners—even most considered successful—have suffered enough abuse and boredom under the harsh prevailing system of mandated schooling forced by those traditional parents and politicians who think they know the answer for *everyone*. They are usually focused on admission to the Yale and Stanford levels of "higher education." Not all youth need or want to finish high school prepared for traditional colleges.

DEFIANT ACTS

Those who consider themselves Visionaries do not need to write more proclaiming the ills of *schooling* and advocating *learning*. Thousands of individuals want to overthrow oppressive education, but *disunited* in the past, they have resorted to the pen, computer, or hot-air voices. Such approaches have failed to garner enough support to force their Traditionalist enemies to negotiate. The overwhelming e-mail and Internet communications among change advocates are mind-boggling—and growing daily. Though intellectual interchanges may be of interest, these dialogues have done nothing to remove the seventh grade. Maybe they will within five years, but not yet; action battle plans, not whispers, are needed NOW!

The immediate attack is to refuse to accept what exists and instead launch greater confrontation and civil disobedience. More Visionaries "who have a dream" cannot continue to "sit in the back of the bus." If events such as Rosa Parks's civil disobedience and the racial murders in Mississippi can lead to the 1964 Civil Rights Act, then critics of the long-controlling establishment can design and demand sensible legislative learning acts for the early 21st-century decades.

In the 1960s and 1970s, the leaders of most education organizations—National Association of Secondary School Principals, National Association of Elementary School Principals, Association for Supervision and Curriculum Development, and the American Association of School Administrators—along with leadership organizations in many states—would not have allowed what happened in the 1980s, 1990s, and 2000s. They spoke out, advocated, lobbied, and engineered innovations. Better teacher organizations supported changes in schooling as long as those involved volunteered.

Unfortunately, in these latter 1980s, 1990s, and naughts, the same schooling "leadership groups" rolled over without a whimper to all the political rhetoric and promise of more money. During the 1960s/1970s period in Minnesota, algebra was not required for high school graduation. In the 2000s, not only was algebra I required, but also algebra II for everyone—both courses with no learning

validity; in fact, the opposite is true. Worse, there was little opposition to this insanity from Minnesota "schooling leaders"—once the
most innovative education state in the nation.

RENEWED OPPOSITION

In the renewal of the WAR against the Traditionalist Army, the
Visionary Army has begun the return to the days when they just
said NO to bad legislation and the lack of options. More leadership,
though, is needed to promote personalized learning before the next
day, not the next century. The Traditionalist "reform rhetoric,"
when applied to all learners, is just old, wrong, and without hope
for a positive future for learning to replace schooling.

Until an increased resumption of the new/old war was declared,
the Visionaries had settled for defeat—or a seemingly agreed-to
truce—as long as they just wrote, but did not act. Thus, most became involved in writing and speaking, directing a small, usually
private, school, a conference of their choir members, or their own
lives; others just tired from lack of progress. They did not unify as
an army of battlefield warriors to resume the fight against learning
injustice. They gave up challenging Traditionalist politicians face-
to-face—with demands to be heard; they only objected with printed
words.

The "political laws," such as No Child Left Behind, required
reading in kindergarten, algebra in high school, and ignorance of
the original—not the current—middle school concept, have all had
negative outcomes. Oppressive controls were passed or allowed to
exist when there was absolutely NO learning research to validate
these decisions.

The conquest of the Visionaries by the Traditionalists was
strengthened under the two Reagan administrations, and continued
through twelve years of the two Bush eras. Ironically Traditional-
ism was allowed to exist under two Clinton cycles, and later by the

Obama/Duncan plans for more national standards and penalties, and misguided legislation. These latter "liberals," looking for votes, only heard the rantings for more and better test scores.

The Visionaries lost the courage of Joan of Arc (1412–1431), who at age nineteen, in the midst of the famed 100 Years War, donned a white suit of armor and personally led the French troops onto the battlefield to victory at Orleans. Later she was captured, declared a heretic, and burned at the stake, but she risked all in defense of her beliefs. Where were the Joan of Arc army members during these many recent decades of oppressive and boring schooling? They certainly were not in the front lines of the battles.

UNFURLED BANNERS

When will learning Visionaries fully unfurl their war banners proclaiming to the politicians that it is the AFFECTIVE DOMAIN that can and eventually may determine a preferable future for education and society? It will not be the COGNITIVE DOMAIN with the testing and limited subject matter requirements. Confluence of the affective, psychomotor, and cognitive is the ideal for human learning and living environments, but if one must be the priority, it is almost always the AFFECTIVE that will influence a positive outcome.

Should not those who consider themselves Visionaries for learning be willing to risk personal sacrifices? Should they not become Vice Presidents for Heresy, and emulating Joan of Arc, don their white suits of armor and openly challenge the wrath of the schooling Traditionalists? Should they not take battlefield action against the ill-grounded policies of misguided and uninformed politicians and "school people"? Should they not enter the fray, become combative, and actually fight for learner choices and options? Should they not overcome the prevailing mentality of the one-size mandates that, on paper, fit ALL?

The nation seems to be intent on reinforcing a failing system at present. It is no use tinkering with our 19th century model of education. It needs to be completely re-thought and restructured. Gradual reform is unlikely to succeed. Radical change is needed.
—Christopher Ball

We need radical re-think in education. Tinkering with a counter-productive system will not do it. Humans invented the current conventional schools over 150 years ago. Therefore, people can now invent new learning modes to replace a system that has outlived its usefulness.
—Roland Meighan

Chapter Three

Communicating Freedom

Democracy means the absence of domination: whilst our model of schooling is riddled with domination, we are clearly on the wrong track, assuming, that is, that we actually believe in democracy.
—Nelson Mandela

Is it not interesting to note that schooling, the institution founded to promote democracy, is now the most undemocratic institution in America?

There is a great lack of total understanding by the public as a whole—including some professed Visionaries—of the need for a combative struggle against traditional schooling and those who support it. The 2010 publication *The Same Thing Over and Over Again: How School Reformers Are Stuck in Yesterday's Ideas* illustrates the factors of poor communication. The book divides opposing armies into two camps: the "Status Quo Defenders" and the "Ineffective New Progressives." Included in the latter are the advocates of "Race to the Top" mentality and the Obama/Duncan plans to finally force "world-class schools."

Both groups are wrong and so are the two classifications! This book goes far beyond *The Same Thing*; those referenced "Defenders" and "Progressives" belong in the same Traditionalist box.

Where are the significantly different and significantly better per-sonalized learning opportunities? Ranking American youth as seventeenth or nineteenth or worse on various world comparison test scores in math, science, and reading offers completely mis-guided information and ignores all the factors involved. Using such test scores, the moneyed power "reform" groups continue to rein-force the Traditionalist Army conquests and obsolete schooling tra-ditions.

Unlike previous privately supported foundations in the 1960s and 1970s (especially Kettering, Danforth, Ford, Mott), the Gates Foundation has not provided money for "start from scratch"—no traditions—to create new learning systems. Their "innovations" have just modified and tried to make better what exists. The slight variations by other groups—as in the Kipp Foundation schools—follow one formula. The Kipp "model" proved to be a little differ-ent but inflexible, regardless of their claims.

None of these more recent Traditionalist groups has reached the level of innovation, experimentation, and research of the 1960s and 1970s and the projects inspired by Federal Title III funding.

A review of the mostly rural society in the early 20th century reminds us that one-room country schoolhouses were usually indi-vidualized. These were better for many students than for those who were forced to enroll in and be bused to consolidated group-paced "modern" school districts!

STRONG TIDES

The desire to turn the tide of the battle is alive, as the Visionary Army has increased its counterattacks against the Army of Tradi-tion. Some progress has been achieved. (Orleans was a victory!) The spirit of Joan of Arc and her followers took 116 years to drive the invaders from French soil. This is a perfect analogy to the problems of the past one hundred years of efforts to drive a wedge in schooling traditions. Can there ever be hope if it takes another hundred years? If the "seventh graders" are in the wrong structure, can allowing even six more years of these students facing the same fallacies be justified? If the seventh grade needs changing, it needs correcting now to free youth otherwise still trapped in a caved-in mine shaft.

Against the control of the financial/political/traditional power structures, the war for learning democracy and freedom of choice has almost been lost. The controllers of the tragedies of schooling have been part of the dominating army. The resistors have too long remained dormant; they now must acquire and utilize stronger weapons of action against the rituals imposed by the conquerors. Citizens have been blind to the fact that the year 2000 arrived with the same system of schooling as existed in 1900. That is akin to basing the current transportation system on the structures designed to accommodate the horse and buggy. Will 2100 arrive with only a "reformed" horse and buggy model?

WRONGED STUDENTS

The Visionary Army has not fought hard enough to free imprisoned learners. Nationwide, 25 percent (on average) are being "pushed out" of schools yearly. In the worst community learning environments, annually 60 to 80 percent are brushed aside or forced into other holding assignments, most commonly wrongly named as "alternative schools." These harsh statistics have been perpetuated by the loud demands for academics and higher test scores, with enforcement by the Traditionalist Army.

Of those learners remaining in this captive system, as evidenced by publicly available data, the percentages are higher or lower in skewed socioeconomic areas—as summarized earlier, 30 percent in "typical" communities receive D/F report cards. They are not enjoying learning. Add to this the 40 percent who receive marks of C;

are they excited to be C students? Seventy percent in required traditional schooling are either failing, unsatisfactory, or mediocre. Of the 30 percent who go on to college and achieve "success" in careers, the majority are bored with their high school classes, requirements, and organizational structures.

In most traditional settings, bells still ring; in 1960 the National Association of Secondary School Principals film *And No Bells Ring* told administrators to silence them. Conformists to tradition yet insist on algebra for thirty-six weeks, when the MIT/Cal Tech high-ability students can pass the national test with a ninety-ninth-plus percentile score in six weeks or less; other college-bound students may need fifty weeks. Is it any wonder the traditional system is not appropriate for the overwhelming percentage of learners?

Increasing numbers of youth and college students are leaving conventional K–12 schooling and four-year university patterns. They seek diverse routes: passing state exit exams early, enrolling in community colleges, participating in independent study programs, joining charter and other forms of alternatives options—including a wide variety of online and distance-learning structures. Limited numbers of fortunate youth partake in home-based education opportunities or the very few national or local personalized college programs.

Good charters and true nontraditional alternatives have helped a little, but most are too small, follow traditional curriculum requirements, and are available to only a handful due to limited lottery selection processes and transportation problems. The successful High School for the Recording Arts in St. Paul, Minnesota, enrolled *only* two hundred dropout, expelled, adjudicated, and homeless youth. Were there not more than two hundred in the Twin Cities deserving of this special opportunity?

Such programs are supported by school boards to remove these "disruptive" students from "regular" classes. What of the other thousands of St. Paul students? The same is true for private choice settings, whether for affluent or lower-income families, but with the added burden of tuition. College and career programs, both public and private, face similar obstacles. The costs have risen astronomically.

> Today, democratic educators continue to struggle on behalf of populations chronically denied their rights and traditionally excluded from meaningful participation in the governing of society.
> —Ron Miller

REACHING LEARNERS

Sadly, in response to the conquests of the public schools by the Traditionalist Army, the Visionary Army further retreated and allowed politicians to eliminate or greatly reduce the best programs of interest for so many learners. These offerings are often the keys to unlocking learning excitement and success, especially for those who are turned off by required biology, or not ready for kindergarten reading.

Essential are full-blown opportunities in art, music, the concepts behind home economics and industrial arts (regardless of their different "new names" in a given state), health, language immersion, drama, business, and similar fields. The best place to help many younger psychomotor-dominant age learners is in home economics, where instead of studying child growth and development or human relations, they concentrate on "baking brownies." As they study the recipes, they are not reading or doing sums; they are *making brownies.* Stir, blend, and mix; one-third cup is fun to decipher.

Personalized physical education programs—not group style throw-out-the-ball in high school period two, or twenty minutes of what is usually only directed recess—are the priorities for so many learners through the interrelationships of the affective and psychomotor domains. Well-prepared specialists in the elementary years have been eliminated, in spite of evidence that the most important traditional school years for personalized instructional physical education are the K–4 levels, followed by 5–8, 9–12, and lastly, athletics. *Hopefully there will be money for all levels including athletes, but if funds are short, the priority must be for K–4 youth.*

It is well known by leaders of the Visionary Army that the best way to reach most all learners—but especially those having difficulty traditionally—is to build their learning programs based upon their strengths and interests. They may spend all day in art—their passion—in the beginning, but they eventually will be willing and want to "learn math," too, and will do so more quickly and better than in the conventional old daily required "math time."

Politicians have erroneously been convinced that to gain election votes, they must focus on the opposite—on the adult perceived weaknesses and failures of the learners. Nothing could be further from the truth related to learning. Why did the oppressed Visionaries not actually fight the war with vigor—not just write—against the enemy army imposing No Child Left Behind (catchy title, but with negative results), especially related to cost benefits?

Expensive state-mandated tests with no significance and misguided curriculum requirements persist. Again the question: why did the modern Joan of Arc leaders and their legions of warriors use the ineffective pen, not direct confrontation? Nationwide test scores have not dramatically improved over the past thirty years under fads such as "rubrics," Race to the Top money, more penalties, and higher required standards.

Moving from the twenty-fifth to the thirty-seventh percentile in a district may be encouraging, but if the mandates of the controlling army are so awesome, why haven't the "world-class programs" reached the eightieth percentiles? They have in a few specialized school situations, but not nationwide! Why after *three decades* of the "push" for higher test scores do the headlines still scream of a "Crisis in Education"?

FADED HISTORY

Most younger potential leaders of the Army of Visionaries—and even many veterans—do not know or have forgotten important educational history; they only remember what exists now. As recently as the 1960s and 1970s, overlooked is the fact that it was the public school optimists who led the then-significant educational-reform efforts. The Free School Movement of this era had a strong effect, but it did not cause major changes in most communities. By contrast, in California in the early 1970s, it was state superintendent of public instruction, Wilson Riles, who called for implementation of the innovative RISE Project (Reform of Intermediate and Secondary Education) as well as elementary school renewal.

To encourage such actions, in the 1960s, Visionary Army leaders and supportive politicians (yes!) succeeded in having Congress pass, and in 1966 Lyndon Johnson sign, Title III. This federally funded national effort was not for more testing, requirements, and world-class status, but instead to sponsor innovation, experimentation, research, and evaluation to determine possible changes that could create significantly better environments for learners. There were exciting and successful programs in most states in the nation. South Dakota, originally trailing in such endeavors, rose to the top with this support.

In addition to the funds from Congress, major contributions came from the Kettering, Danforth, Ford, Chrysler, and other similar corporate foundations to encourage innovation in the public schools. For example, the School Facilities Laboratory, funded by

Ford, provided exciting concepts of new building designs but ironically had even greater influence in encouraging changes in curriculum and instruction.

The election of President Reagan began the demise of these gains by the Visionary Army. The Traditionalist conquerors, in celebrating the victory of the win/lose philosophy—as opposed to win/win—could not understand or accept the 1966 convention-approved platform of the American Association of School Administrators which stated: "We will work for an extended use of all school facilities for educational and recreational purposes."

These traditional "winners" could not comprehend that in good weather, leaving elementary playgrounds—or in bad weather indoor activity spaces—vacant from 8:30 to 10:30 AM made no sense. One could, and still can in most elementary schools, shoot a cannon down the hall during these hours and no one will get hurt. The warden said to the guards: "Do not let the prisoners out of their cells." It is not exercise time, for this is the reading period—even though many learners do better in the afternoon.

Not all students and teachers are hens and roosters; many are nightclub entertainers and do better with later sleep than hearing the early school bus horn waking up the neighborhood—or the 8:30 "tardy bell" in the building. Think, too, of "gifted" secondary students who must be there at 7:30 for the unnecessary extra-period Advanced Placement courses.

In most communities, the same school recreation and instructional spaces are locked for three months in the summer, and are also closed on the weekends, unless for limited hours they accommodate soccer or softball leagues. Such continuing Traditionalist Army policies are wastes of taxpayer expense and opportunities for learning—even though districts howl for more money and "insist" on higher test scores. They do not know how to use effectively what they already have available. Unless there is a huge natural storm, why should playgrounds be empty?

Reorganizing the structure of schooling—for instance eliminating the self-contained elementary classroom organization—is a major forward step. Year-round education programs would increase learning opportunities, and if implemented properly would save districts money. As director of the National Year-Round Association, Charles Ballinger often stated: "If schools in 1900 had adopted a twelve-month nationwide learning calendar, and some group in 2000 wanted to reduce school attendance to nine months, would the public even consider such a change?"

WAR SYMBOLS

The analogies and symbols of the justification for an explosion of the war existing between the Visionaries and the Traditionalists are valid. The infamous 100 Years War has been used principally to cause reflection on the ongoing call to rethink the politics of schooling. The relationship to conflict is further exemplified by reviewing the 1880–1910 period in England.

During these three decades, Edmond Holmes, chief inspector general of schools, enforced very rigid one-size-fits-all curriculum and schooling requirements. After thirty years of rigid practices, he resigned, apologized to the students and parents for hurting so many, and vowed to spend the remainder of his time trying to undo some of the harm he had imposed. In 1911 he wrote *What Is and What Should Be*, followed in 1913 by the famed *Tragedy of Education*, both describing the ills of the state-mandated system of schooling.

Ironically, in this period in the United States, the 1910 Russell Sage Foundation Report found the same or similar tragedies. Will 2113—another hundred years of war—reflect the same one-size mentality, or will the Visionary Army finally counterattack with an all-out offensive? Is it possible that the 14th-century war and the past four hundred years of "schooling" will continue into the 22nd century, or will the reincarnation of Joan of Arc leadership occur? Can the Visionary Army overcome state-imposed rigid schooling—and thus replace the old system with *personalized learning* environments?

Years of planning are not needed. To continue the battlefield theme against schooling, the results of the 1942 Battle of Midway indicated to Visionaries that often "good planning is just dumb luck." The Japanese had planned the attacks on Pearl Harbor and Midway for ten years—designed by the brilliant Admiral Yamamoto and conducted by Vice Admiral Nagumo, who had led the successful attack on Pearl Harbor.

At Midway, with only three days of uncertain planning—and for the Japanese an unbelievable series of discontinuities occurring in their plan—the overwhelming four to one ratio of superior Japanese forces, including four state-of-the-art carriers, lost to a small contingent of U.S. defenders led by two and a half carriers—the Hornet, the Enterprise, and a badly damaged Yorktown. Though the United States lost the men of several heroic dive-bomber squadrons, the four Japanese carriers were sunk, three of them in a six-minute attack. Years of planning do not guarantee success.

TECHNOLOGICAL INFLUENCES

In the decades ahead, traditional schooling structures will be even more obsolete than at present—and certainly than those of the 1960s. However, the present and past contrasts in philosophies are major in the ongoing war. In 1970, with limited computer capacity, the Minnesota Experimental City (MXC) for 250,000 residents was planned without schools—and, of course, then not even cell phones.

Advancing computer capabilities far beyond what exist as websites, blogs, Google, texting, Twitter, YouTube, Facebook, and iPhones are obvious. Long ago Ma Bell corded phones and ringing the operator became museum relics. Yet, most older living citizens used, and were excited over, such magical inventions, and later when the first hundred thousand–dollar computers requiring two air-conditioned rooms were introduced. Even adding area and zip codes was a significant change in communication for them not long ago.

Already online learning, distance learning, face-to-face computers, cell phones, Twitter conversations, virtual schooling, and nationwide conferences without traveling are headed for this same Ma Bell museum. Compared with today, or even 2000, the 1970 "radical" MXC plan for personalized learning, and the earlier 1900 eras pioneering, will seem irrelevant. Remember, movies of the "old West" often show the telegraph eliminating the "new" Pony Express in just twenty years!

The problem with technology and virtual schooling is the continuing need for personal contact in personalized learning environments arranged with people-to-people conversations. Unfortunately, for the foreseeable future, there will be learners who become part of the criminal element; perhaps many can be diverted with individualized approaches and person centers, but with the present understanding of heredity, environment, and association triggers, not all. Programs from either Visionary or Traditionalist approaches cannot guarantee success for 100 percent of learners.

For most people, personalized one-to-one and small-group experiences and interactions are essential. The human touch cannot be replaced by completing all required or optional desired learning via a machine. Future telecommunication weapons will force changes in the battle strategies of the past, but the war between learning and schooling will continue until there is understanding.

In spite of all the atrocities they committed, Germany and Japan became allies of the United States. Hopefully such established new relationships will remain and influence the many continuing conflicts in the global community. The reference to the German and

Japanese atrocities—others have occurred as in recent Darfur or with the Huns of the Middle Ages—has been to reemphasize that often well-educated people committed such horrors.

The new generations in recent enemy countries are striving to prevent reoccurrences of World War II. However, it is extremely difficult to understand and forgive what the Japanese—worse than the Germans—did to brutalize Allied prisoners of war, as well as innocent families and children. Do high test scores prevent massacres?

AFFECTIVE FUTURES

Indicated over and over, the personalized touch related to learning has been, is, and will be—past, present, future—the Visionary priority. Regardless of technology and the importance of the cognitive and psychomotor domains, it is the *affective domain* that can eliminate the current 100 Years War in education, money politics, greed for power, and other ongoing global conflicts.

In schooling, focusing on *cognitive* separate course mandates will only continue business as usual. In learning, the *affective* holds the promise for a far preferable future.

> Students do not participate in choosing the goals, curriculum, or manner of instruction. This is in striking contrast to all the teaching about the virtues of democracy.
> —Carl Rogers

> There must be in the world many parents, like myself, who have young children they are anxious to educate as well as possible, but are reluctant to expose them to the dulling effects of "tell and test them" schools.
> —Bertrand Russell

Chapter Four

Startling Research

A different and better system of appraising and reporting student
progress is essential in a school for everyone.
— J. Lloyd Trump

OPPOSING VIEWPOINTS

In wars of violence, moderation by opposing factions may be ideal,
but seldom attainable. In the wars of politics, compromise is almost
as difficult. Battles of words and votes among parties are anticipat-
ed; most outcomes result in minimal benefits for all citizens—
winners or losers.

In educational debates, as with politics, supporters of opposing
views manage to twist arguments and research results. Groups and
individuals somehow interpret conclusions as evidence confirming
their own positions. The internal response by those unwilling to
bend is common: "Don't confuse me with the facts; my mind is
made up."

The Traditionalist Army of politicians and school people demand "beyond irrefutable proof" when there is a challenge to establishment procedures. Presentations from Visionary Army leaders
stating that nontraditional personalized approaches are better for

the majority of learners are refuted or ignored. Conversely, the Visionaries protest that the long-held conventional schooling structures have NO research support; the common rituals only ease administration and evaluation of the masses.

PROOF POSITIVE

There is no proof that the traditional practices of the past 100 Years War against learning are correct. A few easy examples include the following:

1. What proof is there that the first, second, third, fourth, fifth grade level organization with boxes fitting twenty-five to thirty youth with one teacher all day long is best for ALL learners?
2. What proof is there that "report cards" improve learning for ALL?
3. What proof is there that ALL high school students benefit from required algebra?
4. What proof is there that starting traditional reading instruction for ALL students in kindergarten is the correct age?
5. What proof is there that ALL university students benefit from one required laboratory science?
6. What proof is there that the period 1-2-3-style scheduling is the best organization for ALL secondary students?

The irony is that there are few conclusive answers regarding the best approaches for every person; there is more "proof" than not that most nontraditional learning environments are better suited for the majority of learners.

The recent renewal of the 100 Years War by the Visionary Army was motivated by the fact that the Traditionalist Army refused to acknowledge and accept diversity and options for all learners. The fact remains that there is no research confirming the validity of the Traditionalist positions and their mandated oppressive schooling structures.

AVOIDING CONFLICT

The Traditionalist Army could avoid attacks if it would accept modifications of rigid demands. Unfortunately, the conquerors have not been willing to listen; instead they have reaffirmed their archaic policies through newly minted revisions of "school reform." President Obama, in his 2011 memorial address for the victims of the shootings in Tucson, Arizona, called for humility. He said it was time to stop petty political bickering. Humaneness by both the Visionaries and Traditionalists could lead to the end of the educational war and lead to choices of learning environments best suited for each individual.

The need for humility is witnessed through the debates over the causes of autism, a condition that handicaps afflicted learners. The United States gives, on average, thirty-six medical shots to children; commonly, those injected at thirteen months old include six of the thirty-six in one dose. Denmark has a better health record and less autism, adjusted for their population, yet they give children only twelve injections. The thirty-six illness-prevention shots given in the United States have been tested for safety one at a time by the pharmaceutical companies—not in a variety of combinations.

There is growing controversy over the possible relationship to autism of the three-in-one MMR (measles, mumps, rubella) injection. The American Academy of Environmental Medicine is not opposed to these, but has long opined that the MMR compounds should be given separately over three years. The rates of autism appear higher among those children who receive the three-in-one dose, as opposed to those receiving them one at a time. The University of California–Davis MIND Institute is using an Infant Start Program of six- to thirteen-month-old babies to further study causes and treatments of autism.

Meanwhile, the Traditionalist Army usually gives parents no choice: Take the MMR or, in most states, children are not admitted to schooling. Controversy exists over research studies. Is it not time for both sides to practice humility rather than the dogmatist creed: "In controversial moments, my perception's rather fine; I always see both points of view, the one that's wrong—and mine."

RESEARCH CENTERS

Needed in education are research and development (R and D) centers for learning. The model can be adapted from NASA, including worldwide cooperation as in the international space station. A change in perception is required; there are many unknowns related to how people learn. To transform from schooling to learning—assuming the goal is desirable—communities must be disoriented before being oriented. Citizens must unlearn traditional schooling structures before they can learn to implement better education systems. Research is a key in the effort to unlock the future of perceptions and practices, whether innovative or conventional.

Visionary Army members admit there are almost no absolute studies supporting their causes. However, these rebels against the Traditionalist Army know that there is exhaustive research that can help uproot ancient educational rituals. Studies contradicting conventionalism have been ignored, refuted, hidden from parents, or neglected by the hardcore Traditionalists.

These defenders of schooling claim that the conclusions of many studies are based on results from 19th- and 20th-century students; they do not relate to learners of the 21st century. Nothing could be further from the truth. Traditional politicians and school people who control most news outlets do not want these reviews on the front page, for then the Visionaries could expose the fallacies of their one-size-fits-all mentality.

To illustrate the need for research and development centers, and to expose already validated knowledge, several samplings of older—but crucial for Visionaries to know—research studies are presented. The review begins with perhaps the most important among those ignored by the Traditionalists—a 20th-century investigation conducted by the best education researchers in the nation.

EIGHT YEARS

The Eight-Year Study[1] was launched in April 1930, when two hundred educators met in Washington, D.C., to create a research design that was implemented in September of 1933. It involved thirty, by reputation, well-regarded high schools and three hundred well-recognized universities—the latter of which agreed to exempt graduates of the thirty high schools from the usual higher education entrance requirements. As part of the blueprint, approximately fifteen hundred students from the experimental schools were paired with fifteen hundred youth from nonexperimental schools and matched by gender, age, intelligence, family background, and other influencing factors.

In 1930, in preparation for the study, evaluations were conducted of students in conventional schools. The findings were clear:

1. Most graduates were not competent in the use of the English language.
2. The majority seldom read and were judged unable to express themselves effectively in speech or writing.
3. The teachers, as a whole, were not well equipped for their responsibilities.

4. The principals worked hard but had no real measure of whether they had met the academic objectives, affective needs, and personal interests of their students.

Over eight decades later, and into the new millennium, critics of education continue to make similar statements.

In the actual Eight-Year Study, the experimental schools used a variety of techniques: schools-within-schools, student-teacher advisor systems, student groupings based on mutual interests, written reports of progress rather than traditional report-card letters or numbers, team planning, independent study, a focus on learning how to learn rather than on content, and interrelated curriculum. In science it was difficult to recognize a conventional course on chemistry, physics, or biology, as these were taught interdependently. There were few requirements; students spent much time in the community.

In 1942, when the Eight-Year Study evaluations were completed, the conclusions were evident:

1. Graduates of the experimental schools were not handicapped in their college work.
2. Major departure from traditionally required subjects did not lessen the readiness of the student.
3. Youth from the schools deviating most from the traditional achieved distinctly higher results.
4. The strict requirement of certain subjects was no longer tenable.
5. The assumptions of conventional college-entrance criteria should be abandoned.
6. Students could be trusted with greater degrees of freedom.
7. The courses taken in high school had no relationship to success in college and later life.

The outcomes further reflected that the experimental students did as well as or better than the traditional students related to college grades, participation, critical thinking, aesthetic judgment, and knowledge of contemporary affairs. Additional analysis proved even more startling. When students from the six most experimental high schools of the thirty were compared with students from traditional schools, there were great differences in college attainment in favor of the experimental programs.

The two most extremely nontraditional programs—those with extensive learning in the community, outside volunteers working with students, advisor-advisee systems, students teaching other students, interdisciplinary problem-solving curricula, and flexible use of time—were then selected for comparison with the learners from traditional-format programs. Graduates of these two open-ended schools were found to be "strikingly more successful."

One of the thirty secondary-level programs involved in the Eight-Year Study was the Ohio State University Laboratory School. The students who graduated in 1938 wrote a book titled *Were We Guinea Pigs?*[2] In 1961, a follow-up study of the students was reported in *Guinea Pigs Twenty Years Later*. After two decades, the study found that the "guinea pigs" had been highly successful in life.

The nontraditional-program students were later compared with subjects in the Lewis Terman study of genius and with graduates of Princeton University. The experimental-school graduates were considered more successful by expressing satisfaction with life, being judged as leaders in their professions, leading more stable family lives, possessing better self-attitudes, and being mentioned more frequently in the *Who's Who* publications. Though the study occurred in the 1930s era, the results were not published until 1942; they were unfortunately ignored in most schools during the more important World War II realities.

CONTINUING EVIDENCE

The eight-year analysis was only one of the experimental plans of the first decades of the 20th century. Others included those at the University of Chicago Laboratory Schools led by John Dewey, and the Dalton and Winnetka Plans. Additional reports included the elementary school level. A later study was conducted at the Wilson Campus School of Minnesota State University, Mankato, from 1968 to 1977.[3] It involved students from preschool through grade twelve, and college teacher education undergraduate and graduate programs. Wilson reinvented and went beyond the deviations of the original eight-year experimental schools and applied them to all levels of achievement and age groups, including special education and youth on probation.

After four years of refusing to give tests or institute requirements, the school relented and participated in a Minnesota State Department study. The Wilson students had the highest test scores in the district, while representing a cross section of every school in Mankato. The program was completely nongraded; kindergartners, seventh graders, seniors, and college students were mixed together in curriculum, facilities, philosophies, and choices. Wilson successfully applied the Eight-Year Study to elementary and middle levels as well as to secondary learners.

Eight-Year Study results were also applied to college students. Undergraduate teaching majors who participated at Wilson took no education classes. They learned to "teach" by guiding students. During the four years required for a teaching degree, students could take three years of liberal arts and science courses in the Experimental College at Minnesota State, which was also based on the Eight-Year Study. At the master's and education specialist levels, they could complete their work in a similar "eight-year" manner.

Minnesota State offered a North Central Association accredited master's degree in experiential education—forty-eight quarter hours with no requirements; their personalized program needed only approval by three graduate faculty members, and completion of their individual study plan. The degree continued to be offered after the Wilson era, but unfortunately with numerous traditional modifications. The Wilson K–12 and college programs have been archived in Memorial Library, Minnesota State University.[4]

The 2010 book *Academically Adrift: Limited Learning on College Campuses* (Arum and Roska) was based on a report from the 2007 Collegiate Learning Assessment. The authors concluded that (1) after two years of college those entering comparatively at the 50th percentile had increased only to the 57th; (2) African-American students improved at a rate lower than Caucasians; (3) students out of college for one year were not easily finding work; (4) it was common for students to be in debt fifty thousand dollars; and (5) boosting graduation rates and federal accountability mandates were not of significant value.

FURTHER PROOF

There are additional findings at the elementary level. An international study of mathematics achievement concluded that students who began math at age eight, rather than six, caught on more quickly and had fewer negative attitudes toward math, self, and school.[5] The famous *Plowden Report* indicated that students who had part of their primary schooling in the bomb shelters in England during World War II did better than comparative prewar students who had traditional lesson plans, books, and schoolrooms.[6]

The study by John Goodlad, *Behind the Classroom Door*, found that traditional classrooms were inadequately using accepted principles of learning.[7] The Goodlad and Anderson publication, *The Nongraded Elementary School*, illustrated that nongraded mixed-age classrooms made more sense than classrooms organized by age and grade.[8] In an affluent New York suburban district, every traditional school was given 35 percent more money each year for three years; there was no difference in student achievement.[9]

Paulo Friere helped Brazilian peasant adults learn beginning reading in thirty hours.[10] In a related review, the ability to read was identified as a talent, as in music. The conclusion reached was that comprehension of acceptable reading skills could occur anywhere from ages three to fourteen, depending upon the individual.[11] It has long been known that scores on achievement tests are very stable. Considerable reduction in time spent on reading, math, and spelling did not reduce achievement scores.[12]

An interesting university-level investigation concluded that there were no differences between graduates of liberal-arts-oriented colleges and those of technology-oriented universities in their values and views of life.[13] At the secondary level, Philadelphia teachers in some schools were on strike for eight weeks; other comparable schools stayed open. It was found that students who missed the two months of "schooling" during the strike did as well in end-of-the-year tests as those who had been in school.[14]

These findings were similar in outcome to a Fordham University experiment that permitted some students to skip grades seven and eight and enter the university after four years of secondary schooling. Those students did as well in college as those who completed the traditional six years. Many other recent examples can be cited, including the many who skip traditional grades ten, eleven, and twelve, attend community college for two years, and graduate from a good university with an "academic" major *without a high school diploma* . These reality experiences mirror those of many youths who have managed to escape the "wonderful and essential world-class curriculum."

UNIFORMITY OPPOSITION

The Visionary Army uses validated information to support the concept of choice. It challenges uniform, conventional school proponents to produce similar studies. Traditional Army reports conclude that those who have taken algebra, geometry, foreign language, and chemistry in high school do well in college. Most are already "college prep students." More important, many same or similar courses are repeated; if students pass them in high school, they can complete them in college, too! Successful repetition does not indicate specific classes for everyone—including those preparing for university entrance. The Eight-Year Study clearly refuted this notion.

In a related investigation, the American College Testing Service examined numerous purported university and life success factors:

1. Achievement in cocurricular activities.
2. High grades in high school.
3. High grades in college.
4. High scores on the American College Test (ACT).

The only factor useful in predicting success in higher education and later in life was achievement in cocurricular activities. [15] The same proved true in outcomes using the Scholastic Aptitude Test (SAT). [16] In a different survey, Project Talent interviewed thirty-year-old persons twelve years after secondary school graduation. The analysis of the interviews suggested that a conventional high school education, as a whole, "serves no useful purpose." [17]

The fallacy of uniform structures for ALL students is further proclaimed by citing one of the most amazing facets of education history. The *Carnegie Unit*, for decades the basis of high school credits, originated from a ten-million-dollar Carnegie grant to investigate how to provide college professors a pension. [18] Institutions wanting Carnegie money were told to enroll only those who had fourteen "credits."

This figure was the outcome of accidentally discovering that most secondary-level students were in a class subject 120 hours each year—which was then equated as one "Carnegie Unit." Within five years, the overwhelming majority of 9–12 school districts subscribed to this "pension plan for college professors" by requiring sixteen Carnegie Units for graduation without any educational validity.

More revealing reviews exist. In one, students made gains in reading after "remedial instruction." Within a year, these gains had disappeared; the children made only the progress expected without remedial instruction.[19] A study of colleges accepting every applicant, disregarding high school diplomas, found that those without diplomas had a college grade point average of 2.56 compared to 2.51 for all students. When the data were corrected for age, gender, marital status, veteran status, and family income, the outcomes were the same: nongraduates from high school were doing as well as or better than graduates.[20]

Another investigation looked at factors that make a difference in achievement. Only three were found valid for students:

1. Their feeling of self-worth.
2. Their feeling of control over their own destiny.
3. Their socioeconomic background.[21]

Exciting research has been ignored by Traditionalists who find uniformity much easier to control and administer than diversity. By 1922, a major study involving six diverse communities nationwide proved that homogeneous grouping did not improve achievement, but did create negative social effects.[22] In spite of this, close to 90 percent of the school districts continued some form of homogeneous grouping. Related to these observations, researchers found that under the traditional lockstep system, student attitudes toward school subjects become increasingly negative in a single year; they confess to a sense of dullness and boredom in the daily classroom.[23]

FURTHER CONVICTIONS

It is little wonder that a dissertation survey completed at the University of Nebraska confirmed that high school students from five Midwestern states had negative attitudes toward schooling. When asked if any teacher really cared about them, one-third said "no," one-third said "I think so," and only one-third responded "yes." Not surprisingly, 80 percent of 300 of the *Eminent Personalities of the Twentieth Century*, people as diverse as Albert Einstein and Artie Shaw and all talented, selected the phrase "loathed school" when interviewed regarding their formal education.

To change this situation, summaries have concluded that help was not to be expected from traditional teacher-education programs; the results documented that candidates were required to learn what was in the text and thus become versions of their older professors, most of whom supported a simple concept of curriculum: a prescribed pattern of courses covering topics considered prerequisites for later courses. Conventional credential programs do not help improve the learning system. [24]

Visionary Army leaders never incorporate the term "alternative education," nor is there support for programs that cater only to the few and leave the rest in "regular education." However, one of the conclusions in a study by the Educational Research Service stated: "In almost all cases reviewed, alternative schools were successful in the affective domain." By large majorities, students who chose to attend programs of choice continued to prefer them to traditional schools. Positive student reaction to freedom from petty rules and regulations, and to the closer relationships shared with teachers, was frequently noted. "Student attitudes, attendance, and school climate improved in alternative schools." [25]

In 1993, the California State Department of Education published *Beyond Retention: A Study of Retention Rates, Practices, and Successful Alternatives.* [26] The report was conclusive that retention in education is counterproductive, as were two-year kindergarten and first-grade structures. Students retained did less well than promoted matched counterparts; they were 30 percent more likely to drop out of school by the ninth grade. A related 2000 study by the California Educational Research Cooperative (CERC), University of California–Riverside, found that retention of students in elementary grades increased the likelihood that they will drop out of school; retention did not raise their achievement levels.

A further national review on grade-level retention and school dropouts concluded that repeating a grade provided few remediation benefits and, in the long run, placed students at a higher risk of dropping out of school.[27] The practice of retention continues in a rampant manner. The Visionaries ask "Why?"

MEDFORD STUDY

A major longitudinal study on individual differences, directed by Dr. H. Harrison Clarke, was conducted by the School of Health and Physical Education at the University of Oregon. Medford Oregon public school boys were evaluated at various ages over a period of twelve years. A total of seventy-nine graduate theses—fifty-seven doctoral and twenty-two master-level studies—were completed, focusing on maturity, physique type, body size, gross strength, and relative strength. The spread of individual development was remarkable at each age tested: seven, nine, twelve, fifteen, and seventeen. These differences affected not only physical performance but academic achievement and personal-social relations.

In this Medford study, reaction time was determined to be an independent variable, not interwoven with speed, strength, or other physical factors as first suspected. As a result, coordinated with studies by Little League baseball, the pitching mound for these young players was moved back ten feet and helmets were required. Fourteen-year-old (physiologically) boys were pitching against ten-year-olds in the early-season games.

More important for learning as a whole was the documentation that there is a six-year physiological spread among "seventh graders." Some are "fifth grade" in development, while others are "ninth graders" and almost ready for the National Football League. Only 15 percent were at the average seventh-grade level. "Academic" test scores for these same students ranged from grade three to grade thirteen.[28] This research proved that learners should not be categorized by age—yet more than 90 percent of the Traditionalist Army schools follow some form of rigid seventh-grade grouping and curriculum.

FORGOTTEN WEAPONS

As illustrated, most of the research supporting the Visionary Army has been available for decades, but has lain dormant. The earth-shaking *Twenty-Fourth Yearbook of the National Society for the Study of Education* was presented at the February 1925 annual conference.[29] In two volumes, Part I and Part II, the focus was on "Adapting the Schools to Individual Differences," not on issues such as the illogical current mandated group state tests. The publications were directed by the pioneering Carleton Washburne, superintendent in Winnetka, Illinois, and creator of the famed 1917 *Winnetka Plan*. The underlying philosophy of learning in his individualized, ungraded Winnetka curriculum sought—through physical, emotional, social, and intellectual education—the development of the whole child!

The yearbook included the study completed during six years (1916–1922) in six districts nationally, consisting of three more affluent, high achieving, and three less affluent, lower achieving educational communities. This six-year nationally representational study determined without doubt that homogeneous grouping was of no value academically and hurt students socially. Why then are many "modern" current districts yet using some form of this structure?

One of the outstanding reports in this *Twenty-Fourth Yearbook, Part II,* was presented by Stuart Courtis, professor at the Detroit Teachers College. It stated: "The Detroit study results prove conclusively that, whether instruction is individualized or not, children of each level of intelligence—as shown by scores on mental tests— have a wide range of achievement and very different rates of progress in any specific skill." In one related research study based upon the Detroit First-Grade Group Intelligence Test, the time required by individual children to finish the series of reading lessons was proven to range from twelve to seventy-seven days. How can the same first grade program be assigned to all?

From 1910 to 1930, the Detroit Public Schools were national pioneers, especially in evaluating experimental results in education. The significant spread within each group in many similar studies proved that neither exceptional children, nor any other group of students, fit into a homogeneous class learning at the same rate.[30] Why does ability grouping remain common—as in the harder homework-oriented Advanced Placement courses? As early as 1919 in Dalton, Massachusetts (the program was moved to New York City in 1922), Helen Parkhurst created the progressive *Dalton Plan* which tailored the curriculum to the interests, needs, and abilities of each individual student.[31]

In 1988, another validation of wrong practices for "ability grouping and tracking" was led by Paul George of the University of Florida. Overwhelming evidence illustrated that:

1. It is almost impossible accurately and fairly to place students.
2. Tracking and ability grouping do not result in higher achievement for most students.

3. Tracking produced no positive results in personal or social effectiveness.[32]

Earlier, a 1970 study by the Center for Educational Improvement, University of Georgia, "Ability Grouping: Status and Impact" by Findley and Bryan, concluded that "traditional forms of ability grouping should not be used."

Related to tracking outcomes, a 2010 study in Nashville by staff at Vanderbilt University determined that merit pay and bonuses for teachers produced no better results on standardized tests than among students taught by teachers receiving only the standard contract salaries.[33]

WHAT NEXT?

This small sampling of research supporting Visionary Army goals can be easily multiplied. Traditionalist Army educators are frequently prisoners of their past experiences and have difficulty accepting optional nontraditional programs. Facilitating the learning of young people is hard work, but the major barrier to choices for all learners lies in the states of mind of Traditional Army leaders. Research justifies the Visionary Army demands for a change in the structure of schooling. Through learning—not schooling—dramatic improvement can occur in opportunities and outcomes for students in the public and private schools throughout the democratic nations of the world.

To accomplish the task, ACTION is required by the Visionaries. It is time to implement the changes once thought of as only impossible dreams! The majority of these cited studies reflect what has been wrong with past schooling, and what is still wrong in the present, for the research has been ignored. Looking at future research, what might be discovered to improve the world of LEARNING?

Uniformity is just plain bad education. The tendency of the examination system to arrest growth, to deaden life, to paralyze the higher faculties, involves schooling in an atmosphere of unreality and self-deception which obscures the true purpose of education. Conscription-based schooling and uniform curriculum imposed by adults on children is an affront to learning.
—Edmond Holmes

My ignorance has seldom gotten me into trouble, but I have known so many things that are not so, that I have always been in trouble.
—Mark Twain

NOTES

Grateful acknowledgement is offered to Wayne Jennings, St. Paul, Minnesota, for his contributions to this chapter. Dr. Jennings created the famous St. Paul Open School, based upon the principles of this summarized and continuing research. Jennings has been one of the true Visionaries!

1. Aiken, Wilford, *Story of the Eight-Year Study* (five volumes), Harper & Brothers, New York, 1942. See also a more recent single booklet, *The Eight-Year Study Revisited: Lessons from the Past for the Present,* National Middle Schools Association, Columbus, OH, 1998.

2. Willis, Margaret, *Guinea Pigs Twenty Years Later*, Ohio State University Press, Columbus, OH, 1961. See also Class of 1938, *Were We Guinea Pigs?*, Henry Holt, New York, 1938.

3. Glines, Don, *Creating Educational Futures: Continuous Mankato Wilson Alternatives*, National Association for Year-Round Education, San Diego, CA, 1995.

4. Wilson Campus School Documents, University Archives, Memorial Library, Minnesota State University, Mankato, 2000. For a complete analysis of the procedures and outcomes of the Wilson Campus School, see Long, Kathleen, *Teacher Reflections on Individual School Restructuring: Alternatives in Public Education*, five hundred-page dissertation, University of Oregon Library, Eugene, 1992. Dr. Long spent three years extensively double-blind interviewing over forty Wilson staff members to document the history of this most experimental public research program.

5. Husen, Torsten, *International Study of Achievement in Mathematics*, Vol. 2, Almquist & Wilsells, Uppsala, Sweden, 1967.

6. Central Advisory Council for Education, *Children and Their Primary Schools* (two volumes), Her Majesty's Stationery Office, London, 1967. See also Weber, Lillian, *English Infant School and Informal Learning*, Prentice-Hall, Englewood Cliffs, NJ, 1971.

7. Goodlad, John, *Behind the Classroom Door*, Wadsworth Publishers, Belmont, CA, 1970.

8. Goodlad, John, and Robert Anderson, *The Nongraded Elementary School*, Harper & Row, 1959. See also Anderson, Robert, and Barbara Pavan, *Nongradedness: Helping It to Happen*, Technomics Press, Lancaster, PA, 1992.

9. Martin, John, and Charles Harrison, *Free to Learn*, Prentice Hall, Englewood Cliffs, NJ, 1972.

10. Brown, Cynthia, *Literacy in Thirty Hours*, Expression Printers, London, 1975.

11. Postman, Neil, "The Politics of Reading," *Harvard Educational Review*, May 1970.

12. Beatly, Bancroft, *Achievement in Junior High School*, Harvard University Press, Cambridge, MA, 1932.

13. Jacob, Phillip, *Changing Values in College*, Harper & Brothers, New York, 1957.

14. Lytle, James, and Jay Yanoff, "The Strike Effects (if any) of a Teacher Strike on Student Achievement," *Phi Delta Kappan*, December 1973.

15. Munday, L. A., and J. C. Davis, *Varieties of Accomplishment after College: Perspectives on the Meaning of Academic Talent*, ACT Research Report No. 62, American College Testing Service, Iowa City, IA, 1974. See also Hoyt, D. P., *Relationship between College Grades and Adult Achievement: A Review* of *the Literature*, ACT Research Report No. 7, 1965.

16. Wallach, Michael, "Psychology of Talent and Graduate Education," International Conference on Cognitive Styles and Creativity, Graduate Record Examination Board, Montreal, November 1972.

17. Gagne, Robert, "Project Talent," *The School Administrator*, American Association of School Administrators, February 1976.

18. Tompkins, Ellsworth, and Walter Gaumnitz, *Carnegie Unit: Its Origin, Status, and Trends*, Education and Welfare Bulletin No. 7, U.S. Government Printing Office, Washington, DC, 1954.

19. Silberburg, Margaret, and Norman Silberburg, "Myths in Remedial Education," *Journal of Learning Disabilities*, April 1969.

20. Feldstein, Donald, "Who Needs High School?" *Social Policy*, May/June 1974.

21. Coleman, James, et al., *Equality of Educational Opportunity*, Superintendent of Public Documents, Washington, DC, 1967.

22. Washburne, Carleton, ed., "Adapting the Schools to Individual Differences," *Twenty-Fourth Yearbook*, National Society for the Study of Education, 1925. Also published by Public School Publishing Co., Bloomington, IN, 1929.

23. Neale, D. C., et al., "Relationship between Attitudes toward School Subjects and School Achievement," *Journal of Educational Research*, Vol. 63, 1970.

24. Taylor, Harold, *The World as Teacher*, Doubleday, Garden City, NJ, 1969.

25. Educational Research Service, *Evaluations of Alternative Schools*, Research Brief, Educational Research Service, Arlington, VA, 1977.

26. George, Catherine, ed., *Beyond Retention: A Study of Retention Rates, Practices, and Alternatives*. California State Department of Education, Sacramento, 1993.

27. Roderick, Melissa, "Grade Retention and School Dropout," Research Bulletin No.15, *Phi Delta Kappan,* December 1995.

28. Clarke, Harrison, ed., "Individual Differences, Their Nature, Extent, and Significance," *President's Council on Physical Fitness Research Digest*, Washington, DC, October 1973.

29. Washburne, Carleton, ed., "Adapting the Schools to Individual Differences," *Twenty-Fourth Yearbook*, National Society for the Study of Education, 1925. Also Published by Public School Publishing Co., Bloomington, IN, 1929.

30. Courtis, Stuart, "Data on Ability-Grouping from Detroit," *Twenty-Fourth Yearbook*, Part II, National Society for the Study of Education, 1925.

31. Parkhurst, Helen, *Education on the Dalton Plan*, Dutton, New York, 1922.

32. George, Paul, "What's the Truth about Teaching and Ability Grouping Really?" *Teacher Education Resources*, Gainesville, FL, 1988.

33. Springer, Matthew, "Merit Pay and Teacher Bonuses," *National Center on Performance Incentives*, Vanderbilt University, Nashville, TN, 2010.

Chapter Five

Looking Forward

It is not because things are difficult that we do not dare. It is because we do not dare that they are difficult.
—Lucius Seneca

THINK GLOBALLY

Most people do not understand why it is critically important to look ahead. We know in our hearts that we are in the world for keeps, yet we are still tackling twenty-year problems with five-year plans, staffed with two-year personnel, working on one-year appropriations. It is simply not good enough. It explains why we lurch from crisis to crisis. It will not be easy to change the present mindset, which focuses on short-term fixes for long-term problems—but change it we must.

Harlan Cleveland, former president of the World Future Society, presented these thoughts as he examined the growing global dilemmas—a series of micro-problems that add to one *macro-problem*—to be solved interdependently; if not, there is great expectation for a gloomy future. Education is one of the micro-problems. The traditional mind-set of schooling is the reason why education continues to lurch from crisis to crisis. Fellow futurist and inventor of the geodesic dome, Buckminster Fuller was a proponent of this theory, but he expressed it differently. He stated that the future holds the potential for a Golden Age, but only if people change their *lifestyles*, *values*, *priorities*, and *institutions*—the latter of those included the archaic concept of "schooling."

The United Nations realized global leadership, including educational leaders, must look forward if the future is to be "more sunny than more gloomy." From the report *Declaration of the Responsibilities of the Present Generation Toward Future Generations*, part of Article 10 states, "Education is an important instrument for the development of persons and society. It should foster peace, justice, understanding, tolerance, equality, and health for the benefit of present and future generations—to ensure full freedom of choice."

Testing for math and reading scores and closing schools was not part of fostering, but freedom of choice was included. Continuation of the competitive, repetitive, cognitive-focused 19th- and 20th-century schooling systems only widens the 21st-century disparities between those who master the demands of tradition, and those who do not fit the uniform patterns enforced by politicians.

The United Nations' goals for education are lofty. Existing prewar mandated approaches did not prevent the atrocities by the well-schooled Japanese and Germans, nor have these goals affected terrorist organizations or the more recent tragedies of less well-schooled countries such as Iraq, Afghanistan, and Rwanda. These wars do reconfirm that it is the affective—not the cognitive—domain that is the key if ever there is hope for improving global conditions.

The violence in all the wars in history has not been prevented by "education." Learning—if applied globally—may someday make a difference. In the United States, the nonviolent war against learning by the Traditionalists will not be overcome unless the Visionaries attack schooling until there is peace. Part of the solution involves the call in Article 10 of the United Nations for freedom of choice. Achievement of this goal requires thinking globally, but acting locally.

ACT LOCALLY

How can there be new Action that moves *schooling* toward *learning*? Does not the fact that, for the past two hundred years, many millions of people have believed and accepted that rigid schooling validates the prevailing gospel? The idea persists among the masses that tradition supports conventional dogma; these conformists do not listen to their opponents, who state that the present practices are untenable. The Traditionalist Army has controlled schooling by convincing people that the dogmas are not only tenable, but for two hundred years they have been the best way to educate citizens. To improve accepted schooling, the Traditionalists have imposed even stricter requirements.

Visionary Army leaders are more convinced than ever of the need to overcome the long-standing uniform controls. Ironically, Visionaries refer to two fables for children as part of their inspiration and hope. Traditionalist school people see no connection between these stories and learning. Visionaries revel in them, for they *imagineer* the possibilities for the future. Roald Dahl and his friend Willie Wonka stated: "We make dreams out of realities, and realities out of dreams; we are the dreamers of the dreams"—here for the future possibilities for achieving the United Nations goal of freedom of choice through personalizing learning.

Jonathan Swift and Gulliver had even greater vision when they stated: "I have seen what others can only dream. I know these descriptions are true—for I have been there." Visionaries have "been there" by envisioning personalizing learning avenues. In concert with Gulliver and their farsighted Epcot Center friends—Figment and Dreamfinder—they have "been there." Most education leaders who have actually pioneered and implemented various alternatives have "seen" how to go beyond conventional schooling; they have created options for those who have volunteered.

Visionaries believe in the potential for new learning systems. They assert that the assumptions upon which the schooling of yesterday and today are based are no longer valid. In their place is the belief that true education is a lifelong process, unrestricted by age, hours of the day, classroom walls, or technology.

NEW VISIONS

Ronald Barnes envisioned in an edition of the *Forum*, subtitled "Education: New Visions for the Future," learning systems that would replace schooling. The evolving concepts focus on very different sets of assumptions: (1) Learning is life; people never stop learning. (2) Learning occurs everywhere. (3) People can learn on their own. (4) All individuals are important regardless of how much they know. (5) Authority is shared by all. (6) Learning is tailored to meet the needs of each individual. (7) Learners of all ages—beyond infancy—can make their own decisions regarding what and how they should learn. (8) People form positive social networks on their own without required formal schooling.

These concepts are in sharp contrast to those of the Traditionalist Army of politicians and school people who have continued to control based upon conventional assumptions: (1) Learning is preparation for life—living after schooling. (2) Learning occurs primarily in school. (3) Only specialists with credentials can impart knowledge. (4) People with great knowledge are better and more powerful than those with less knowledge. (5) Education occurs in schooling based upon a prescribed curriculum. (6) People seldom learn on their own. (7) Schooling is necessary to socialize people to become civilized and responsible members of the community.

When Traditionalists were forced toward "innovation," they grasped such misunderstood solutions as Outcome-Based Education, which they supported only briefly. Eventually, for most, it became just another form of rigidity.

In one version of potential new learning systems—versus traditional schooling—the community is the primary learning laboratory. Every person is a potential learner, but also a potential resource person for others. The learner is the focus; the process assumes that individual differences must be accommodated. Traditionalist leaders trumpet these ideals, but continuously deny them daily in schooling—evidenced by the massive mandated same-test-for-everyone requirements.

In this envisioned example, there are no schools and no full-time teachers; learning, not teaching, is the central core. One reason that efforts to implement freedom of choice to allow learners to escape schooling is that the ruling Traditionalist Army politicians have been convinced that learning happens only under the direction of "teachers" in schools. Visionary Army leaders leave their versions of "education" open to change. Self-renewal is designed to avoid continuing failings. No learner is excluded, for a system in flux adapts to each individual.

FUTURE PROLOGUE

William Shakespeare once wrote that the past is prologue—to the future. Though no longer basking in the literary glory of the decades of the 1500s, the recent past 20th century is still prologue, as humans speculate on the 22nd century. Many of the children alive in 2015 will witness 2100 AD, unless humankind decides to destroy itself through greed, power, and an unsustainable environment.

One past-is-prologue vision related to living and learning in this current era is found in the *Northwestern Bell Magazine* of 1972. Titled "MXC: A City with a Taste of Tomorrow," the article described plans for the Minnesota Experimental City—a community of 250,000 people built on sixty thousand acres—only ten thousand of which were to be cemented—designed to be a completely new habitat. It was to experiment unlike any previous trials in existing population centers. Like the mythical city of OZ, the MXC was to rise in splendor in the North Country of Minnesota.

The buildings were to be unique and efficient, the society free and open, and the environment unscathed. All the latest technology—people movers, a geodesic dome, pollution control, and village living—were to be utilized. Education (learning) was personalized through use of existing MXC health, business and travel facilities, and beginning life, stimulus, gaming, project, and family-life centers.

The Visionary Army leaders illustrate that it is not hard to create future learning systems through the often-referenced concept of Imagineering. Traditionalist Army leaders reject such "dreaming" as unrealistic. Their opponents ask: Why is it so hard to see what Gulliver saw? Imagineering takes the Visionaries to Lilliput.

What would it be like to live in the MXC—a city for the future? A group of visitors drive toward it; they begin to glimpse the approaching horizon. What can they picture from a distance: skyscrapers, low buildings, or nothing—for all is underground? They reach the road entrance and turn toward the MXC. Their vehicles are hooked to an automated highway that takes them to an automated parking area; no cars are allowed in the core and surrounding residences of the city. A people-mover takes the visitors to the City Center. Now that they have arrived, what do they see—tall buildings, underground entrances, a geodesic dome with year-round climate control, technological centers?

Because this visiting group includes many educators, they look for school buildings. Do they find them, or only community centers, or nothing resembling a "schooling" environment? What would be the format for learning in the most experimental city in the world? Before the MXC "education" design is revealed, in small groups the visiting educators share what they expect to find. For the Visionaries, the hope is that such sharing will lead to convincing the visitors that Traditionalist assumptions regarding schooling are wrong, and thus increase the numbers joining the battle to win freedom of choice for learning.

PLANNED DESIGNS

The MXC was planned during the infancy of technology. Now there are available online schools featuring daily guidance, Advanced Placement courses, individualized pacing of subjects, and diploma options. Unfortunately, most of these developing avenues are based on Traditionalist curriculum, credits, and controls. How does a technological society change the concept of education? For Visionaries, it increases the reality of overcoming Traditionalist suppression, but a war for learning continues. The moneyed power groups yet maintain control; their versions of mandated schooling must be defeated.

In the MXC, though only at the beginning of the technological impact, people were to have been connected via the LORIN— Learning Options Resource Information Network. This was a personalized computer highway for people to find each other to learn with or from, individually or in a group. The chosen topics could be whatever was desired, with options for utilization of special facility centers. The 1972, MXC design was only one of numerous new communities addressing assorted futures.

Tianjin Eco-City in China is planned to be completed in 2020. It will showcase the latest energy-saving wind and solar power technologies, rainwater recycling, desalinization of seawater, and innovative wastewater treatment. Though exciting as one of the many proposed Eco-Cities of the future, little new has been announced for learning. Will the Chinese maintain tight control of their schooling system in such an environment, or will they allow the creation of Visionary learning for the China of 2020–2030?

Not only are Eco-Cities on the horizon, but there is a need to relate learning systems to the burgeoning global human population which is tripling during the lifespan of the reader. With eighty million people added each year, the 2011 global population reached seven billion (Blue Planet United, *Population Press*, Fall 2010). Nine out of ten births occurred in the poorest and most politically unstable regions of the planet. Millions of the present inhabitants are on the move geographically each year, placing greater stress on the existing social and ecosystems. The increasing populations are creating the obvious problems of climate disruption, shortages of food and water, organized violence, and unsustainable consumption practices.

For schooling, the Traditionalist Army of U.S. politicians maintains that all that is needed to overcome such dilemmas are higher test scores, more algebra, and earlier reading. The Visionary Army believes that maintaining a firm hold on Traditional schooling is a suicidal view of the future. The undemocratic values continue to support increasing consumption by the affluent, and ironically the destruction by the poor of valuable forests. The need for caring societies is obvious.

PERFECT STORM

In the 2010 book *World on Edge*, Lester Brown describes how the global community is facing a "perfect storm" of food shortages, water scarcity, and costly oil between 2020 and 2030. The belief is that the threats to the future are not armed aggression, but rather climate change, population growth, water shortages, poverty, rising food prices, and failing states—not to mention personal and corporate greed for profit and power. Reforestation, soil conservation, fishery restoration, universal learning availability, and family planning can address these U.S. and global problems.

The controlling schooling Traditionalists state that such inflammatory words and topics are just scare tactics; societal dilemmas have long occurred or been prophesied, but they note that "schooling" survives. These enemies of learning contend that more math, and closing the achievement gap among readers, provide solutions. They continue to advocate consumption of the traditional curriculum, schooling formats, and purchase of more goods.

The Visionaries declare that too few are working on global sustainability. They believe the Earth, and therefore civilization, are in trouble. The population explosion and overconsumption contribute. There is urgency to eliminate poverty, make space for the remaining animal species, and to work together. They cite a statement by the pioneering Jacques-Yves Cousteau: "We must alert and organize the people of the world to pressure the leaders to take specific steps to solve the two root causes of the environmental crisis including wasteful use of irreplaceable resources. Overconsumption and overpopulation underlie every problem today."

PLANET EARTH

It is easy to understand why there is a War between Traditionalists and Visionaries in education. The former do not see the relationship of these global problems to the day-by-day political schooling system they wish to maintain—but "reform." The task of schooling is to raise test scores to "world-class standards" by forcing early reading, algebra, tests, discipline, and better enforcement against truancy.

Visionaries are convinced that blind continuation of the practices and structures of an archaic system will not make a difference. "Schooling" people do not see a relationship to global survival; Visionaries envision "learning" as a key contribution toward alleviating the world dilemmas, stating that social justice and environmental protection are the most significant issues facing humans today.

The Visionary Army leaders are determined to overcome negative Traditionalists. They believe that through personalized learning systems, learners can study and contribute solutions. Required, they believe, are profound reassessments of values, lifestyles, and curriculum that focus on the preservation of present and future generations. Solving algebraic equations may interest a few, but knowledge of how to apply these solutions is of little value if there is not enough water to live on Planet Earth.

> Self-concept, values, enthusiasm, responsibility, initiative, and acceptance of others are part of the formula for creating powerful principles of learning.
> —Wayne Jennings

TWISTED TALK

In the midst of the worst of the 2011 economic recession, Wall Street mentality tried to convince consumers that there was no accompanying inflation—in spite of multibillion-dollar profits still made by oil companies, and local rising gas and meat prices. One example cited at a community meeting on the economy was the statement that the new iPad 2 was twice as good as the iPad 1 and obtainable at a cheaper price. The session was interrupted by an unemployed mother of two youngsters who shouted, "Yes, but we can't eat iPads!"

The corporate mentality taught in schooling suggests that marketers can charge $5.99 for a product, not $6.00 or $5.80, or a true price value. The advertised product cannot be exactly $5.99 or $14,999. Such pricing may be legal, but certainly unethical, yet such twisted tactics are learned by price manipulators in their classes called "schooling." Consumer advocates state: "Never buy a product with a price ending in 99."

Will future generations of teachers focus on ethical values, or will corporate manipulation by a schooling—not a learning—system continue to be accepted in 2100? Sixteenth-century Don Quixote provides a provocative answer by stating: "When Life itself seems lunatic, who knows where madness lies . . . to surrender dreams . . . may be the madness . . . and maddest of all, to see life as it is and not as it should be."

> What is meant by non-interference of the school in learning? It means granting students the full freedom to avail themselves of teaching that answers what they need and want—not forcing them to learn what they do not need or want. . . . It is not likely that schools based on student freedom of choice will be established even a hundred years from now.
> —Leo Tolstoy

Chapter Six

Insightful Perceptions

My eyes saw what no one should witness: gas chambers built by learned engineers, children poisoned by educated physicians, infants killed by trained nurses, women and babies shot and burned by high school and college graduates. So I am suspicious of education—reading, writing, and arithmetic are important only if they serve to make our children more human.
—Holocaust survivor

MINORITY OPPOSITION

One goal of educational Visionaries is to create better *learning* opportunities for the present and future. This task requires action now. The mission does demand increased support in the ongoing war against the existing practices of schooling. Visionaries have no desire to re-create the past. However, by validating the continuing educational battles, history can assist in envisioning preferable futures. Except for brief periods, efforts have failed to ensure freedom of learning choices. Why?

The war to overcome one-size-fits-all politicians does involve the past and the minority against the majority. Smaller Poland was unable to prevent its conquest by the Germans, but the resistance continued. The Americans on Corregidor could not stop the Japanese, but they fought; for those who surrendered, next was their effort to survive the Bataan Death March. In education, the smaller Visionary Army fought throughout the 20th century; it won some battles, but in the long run, the stronger Traditionalist Army prevailed.

As educators look ahead, it is crucial that they understand the longstanding desires to correct the ills of mandated schooling. The continual criticism by the minority has elevated again the war against tradition. Societal and learning critics throughout the 20th and now the 21st centuries have voiced opposition to the Reagan, Bush, Clinton, Bush, Obama education policies, and to the rigid school people and moneyed foundations who have been bedded with most state and local politicians.

In 2011, middle school and core curriculum leader Gordon Vars commented, "It's a wonder that the visionary leaders have not been taken hostage by the corporate/capitalist monsters who have been warring against everything human and progressive that remains in the public schools." It doesn't take Phi Beta Kappa scholars to recognize the problems created by earlier collapses against what currently exists as education! If there is a sincere desire to release vibrant, excited learners from traps set by legions of Traditionalists, highlights from the past must be reviewed.

BEING TAUGHT

Insightful Perceptions from throughout the 20th century come from many learned scholars—and even the peasant Schoolboys of Barbiana (Italy). In 2011, why were increasing numbers of youths dropping out of schooling? Why were most "gifted" students bored? A glance at a cross section of critics over the past one hundred years provides the answers. Winston Churchill alluded to the problems of traditional schooling when he stated: "I am always ready to learn, but I do not always like being taught."

From the student viewpoint, maybe Lucy perceived it even better when she said to Charlie Brown: "I would like to say I enjoyed this first day at school. I realize the teachers put in much effort, and administrators worked hard to develop our scholastic program. The PTA has also done its share. Therefore I would very much like to say I enjoyed this first day at school! But I didn't!"

The 2010 San Francisco School Board hired private detectives—along with using its own staff time and money—to find and remove over two hundred students in one year (2009) who, according to existing laws, should not be enrolled in San Francisco schools. Why can't students attend public schools of choice when they are enjoying learning and doing well, or for the convenience of working parents? The wrong middle-of-the-street boundaries for dividing lines for school attendance are to ensure financial reimbursement, but also to prevent athletic recruitment for schools to build powerhouse sports programs. Cannot such issues be easily and humanely resolved? The Traditionalists say NO—they hire detectives and truant officers. The Visionaries say YES—they seek to establish realities that provide the best opportunities for the learner. Such divisions—major and minor—reflect "educational" problems in the second decade of the 21st century.

LOOKING BACK

It is helpful to look back one hundred years to observe if there has been progress in improving schooling. A 1910 report seems appropriate to begin reflection. In that year, the Russell Sage Foundation published the results of a survey concerning school attendance.

Last June an army of 250,000 boys and girls averaging 14½ years of age proudly marched from the public schools having completed eight successful years. During the same year, another army of 250,000 children of the same age dropped from the ranks, having failed graduation. The larger fraction of these dropouts had completed only six years of study. . . . This is our great educational problem. It transcends all questions as to scope and content. . . . Because the students have failed, they are humiliated. Their confidence is destroyed, and they are left with the conviction that they are failures.

As a follow-up, the July 1911 *Hampton's Magazine* published an article, "Keeping the Children in School" by Rheta Dorr. She stated: "We are beginning to realize that our public school system, the very basis of American civilization, is not working. . . . It does not educate. The machinery is all there: fine buildings, trained teachers, compulsory attendance laws, books, and accessories. But there is a cog loose somewhere. The children leave school without having been educated."

The Russell Sage survey of 386 larger cities found that only one-fourth of the children finished sixth grade, and only 6 percent graduated from high school. Why? Most could have stayed, but they refused, enduring schooling only until the compulsory age of fourteen. The report stated that similar conditions existed in every city in the United States. The children left because they wanted choices of education that the schools did not provide.

Even in 1910, this study concluded that "we are too prone to accept a situation, continue a system, cling to an ideal, long after it has served its purpose; the schooling system is surrounded with conventionalities." In her one hundred-year-old 1911 article, Rheta Dorr wrote: "In this day and generation, especially in the cities, it is not only futile, it is criminal to allow children to run idle during three months of the year. To put it mildly, it is dangerous to turn them into the streets from three o'clock until dark."

In January 1927, an article in the *Platoon School Journal* by author Stuart Courtis recognized that "an enriched curriculum made possible the modification of academic preparation for life to life itself. In place of studying separate and unrelated subjects— arithmetic, reading, writing—which have no counterpart in life out- side of school, the learner should pursue his or her own interests." Conversely, Traditionalist school authorities have gone the limit in establishing barriers between formal school life and real life out- side the school. Courtis was only one of many Visionaries of the 1920s who recognized that schools then were not functioning as well as desired.

CONTINUED PROTESTS

The 1930s continued protests against the establishment. One of the more interesting articles of this era was written by Lewis Lawes, warden at Sing Sing Prison, published as "A Challenge to the School" in the September 1932 issue of *Good Housekeeping*. War- den Lawes commented:

> The American School System, the finest and most comprehen- sive devised by man, has served the purpose for which it was originally planned. It has reduced illiteracy to a minimum . . . yet as we review the accomplishments, one thing stands out in bold and sad relief. The splendid and costly educational pro- gram that has been the pride of government . . . has done nothing to mold the character of our people. Its insistence on scholastics has left no room for character training. . . . The faults of educa- tion become the problems of penology. The failures of our schools and general educational methods are filling our juvenile homes, reformatories, and prisons.
>
> The seriousness of the situation becomes apparent when the records show that in Sing Sing the educational background is higher today than in the past, and instead of dropping out in the 4th or 5th grade, the average prisoner has completed high

school, and some even institutions of higher learning. . . . There is a missing link between education and character, which the public school system has not been able to discover. In the emphasis on intelligence and brains, often forgotten—or neglected—is the necessity to detect the uses of both.

The era of the 1930s is of particular interest in relation to the present and future 21st-century dilemmas. In the midst of a deep depression, similar but worse than the economic downturn of the 2000 and 2010 decades in America—and globally—the social Visionaries were addressing the decaying conditions in the schools and the related deficiencies of society. They cited that the public had been trying to solve the "youth problem" for twenty years (circa 1915–1935) by creating over forty child welfare agencies— ironically, rather than wider use of the schools.

In an April 1936 sermon at the Riverside Baptist Church in New York City, Reverend Harry Fosdick stated: "Now we walk the city streets and watch the boys and girls . . . we are making criminals faster than we can build jails, for the youth habitually spend their leisure time on the streets . . . for the school system is failing to develop citizens."

In another 1936 report from the University of Michigan, *Education and Social Trends,* Professors Schorling and McClusky stated on pages 58 and 59: "The shifting roles of the church and home demand that the school assume more and more responsibility for the integration of the person. . . . We speak glibly of educating the whole child, an ideal that is admirable but in practice is largely meaningless. . . . Society has deposited the "whole child" in excessive numbers at the desk of the teacher."

EDUCATION ADVOCATES

Education agents of change were also addressing the problems identified circa 1900, but untouched over three decades. In 1845 Boston, records were kept of the total number of students each day who were flogged, and as late as 1936, the sign of the schoolmaster was a bundle of switches. Nineteen thirty-six was a particular year of protest against Tradition.

Professor William Heard Kilpatrick wrote in *Remaking the Curriculum*, the following: "The new curriculum must then put first things first. The child must come before subject matter as such. This is the everlasting and final condemnation of the old curriculum. It put subject matter first and it bent—or if need be broke—the child to fit the system."

Is it any wonder that Visionary Army leaders are finally up in arms again, warring against the Traditionalist Army? The enemy generals have continued to dominate youth by the old disciplines of force and fear: pass the test or no advancement or diploma. It has been a 100 Years War. These 1930 examples are eight decades old, yet the Traditionalists cling to one-size-fits-all policies rather than agree to better approaches allowing for personalized learning systems.

SOCIETAL REALITIES

The existing war is necessary for the Visionaries to change Traditionalist mind-sets. Societal critics who are not in education long have recognized Traditionalist domination. The academically brilliant mathematician and philosopher Bertrand Russell would not only clash with, but would be a leader against, tradition. His 1926 statement in *On Education* is even more relevant now—almost a hundred years later: "There must be in the world many parents, like myself, who have young children they are anxious to educate as well as possible, but are reluctant to expose them to the dulling effects of 'tell and test them' schools."

Visionary Army leaders must address the rapidly changing societal and technological realities of the 21st century. However, they must also know history related to education, and recognize that Visionary views are held by many—not just the author or any one person—and represent long-standing criticisms and perceptions of very insightful people. They should be convinced that it is finally time to heighten the war to overturn current schooling practices, and instead implement personalized learning venues.

Efforts to change tradition continued throughout the 1930s. Had it not been for World War II, the 1940s may have witnessed an uprising against many of the practices of the Traditionalist Army. The Visionary Army was making progress. In the March 11, 1937, *Platoon Magazine*, Arthur Dean wrote: "Every time a child reaching the age of 14 is found by his teacher not to be clever with the hands, or interested in art or music, or capable of being honest, thrifty, hardworking, or proficient in athletics, nature, or some hobby . . . that teacher should be fired or reduced to minimum salary until he or she discovers what each child can do and starts him or her doing it. . . . It would take a good teacher just thirty seconds to declare that every one of the pupils was 'smart in something.'"

It has long been recognized that traditional schooling has not worked for the majority of youth. Another hundred years of what exists—the current test, test insanity toward "world-class standards"—cannot continue. Visionary educational futurists must strike overwhelming blows, this time not only to make short-term gains as with President Johnson and Title III projects, but long-term, ever-improving change for the future. Reform and renewal are words to be eliminated from education vocabulary. Completely new learning venues must in no way reflect schooling. "Schools" are not the future.

GREAT LOCKOUT

To emphasize the point that educational Visionaries trying to change schooling to learning must know the past, the 1907–1937 schools of Gary, Indiana, proved that insightful perceptions can "make dreams out of realities." Such are not idle lines from fables. Reviewing centuries of schooling history is necessary. The process illustrates, through a looking-glass peek into one small era of Americana, that Visionaries have history on their side.

A wonderful booklet, *The Great Lockout in America's Citizenship Plants,* by William Wirt, tells the story of educational developments in Gary, Indiana, from 1907 to 1937. This "old" thirty-year tale is at the same time prologue to the "new" future, for it describes what the Traditionalists would claim as a wild, radical proposal by Visionaries that would be impossible and undesirable to implement. Sadly, the best features of the Gary Plan are not even available in the schooling systems of today.

Wirt himself was a controversial and somewhat dictatorial person. Not only was he superintendent, but he also owned the Nash automobile franchise, was president of the local bank, and invested heavily in real estate. He made cultural mistakes by, for example, originally following community demands to separate African-American students. Professionally, some classrooms were outfitted with inkwell-holder desks bolted to the floor. He was considered arrogant. Though admittedly Wirt was not without fault, the examination of his brilliant innovations and the then "best in America" school system is the focus.

In 1904, as superintendent in tiny Bluffton, Indiana, he implemented the first year-round education plan of the 20th century. His small school was growing in population; the school board would not provide money for expanding the facility. The solution was to create an all-year plan that would address both space and learning for the children of this rural farming community. He was so successful that when the new town of Gary, Indiana, came into existence in 1906—the result of U.S. Steel opening a huge mill with jobs available—he was invited to become the first superintendent of schools.

There, in 1907, Wirt created the famous Work-Study-Play curriculum and the first Platoon System! He wrote: "Thirty million American children are locked out of their schools for one half the time they should be used. Thirty million adults who want to use the schools are locked out practically all of the time. Gary broke this lockout (of America's citizenship plants) in 1907 by extending the use of its schools."

The Platoon System was unique in relation to space and thus curriculum. In the morning, half the students were in rooms designed for the usual reading, mathematics, and history studies. The other half were in the fun electives—science, languages, art, music, print shop, physical education, home economics, and more. Then, in the afternoon, the groups switched, so the elective-class students went to the "basic" studies, while the other half went to the electives programs.

By building only half the usual traditional classrooms, he spent the saved money on special facilities. As the years progressed, the Gary schools had two swimming pools (boys and girls), two gymnasiums, extended play facilities, as in handball courts, and special rooms, as in science laboratories. All this was at the same cost—or less—of comparable Indiana districts. Great use was made of off-campus community buildings and outdoor locations, such as ponds and wildlife preserves.

MODEL PROGRAM

The curriculum of the Work-Study-Play plan was unique in that during the eight-hour school day, the students studied for two hours (reading and all), "worked" for two hours for career preparation and interest (print shop, welding, foreign language, science, home economics), and spent two hours in play (instructional physical education, recreation activities, and animal and farm studies). One hour was allotted for a nourishing lunch, and one hour for "free play." These time allotments varied.

The Gary students scored better on comparative state tests at less cost, yet the schools were open twelve hours a day, six or seven days a week, for fifty weeks of the year. The programs were open to adults who primarily used the facilities after work to learn English, share learning with their children, or for recreation—as in use of the swimming pools. The concept was a "child's center in an adult world." The students had multiple "teachers," used the entire community as a "school," and "learned" round-the-year.

To encourage students to go beyond eighth grade, Wirt expanded the high school offerings, began a community college, and eventually convinced Indiana University to open a satellite campus in Gary. He prevailed over the opposition to create these improvements. Testament to his conviction that the Gary schools were going to offer learning for everyone year-round is the fact that today Indiana University Northwest is located in Gary—the eventual result of his thirty-year leadership.

Is the Gary program a model for the 21st century? No! But such innovation from 1907–1937 proves that changes in education can be achieved and schooling can become learning. Unfortunately the Gary concepts, which served every family background—Italian, German, Polish, Mexican, Jewish, African, Asian, Confederate and Yankee—all of whom came to work in the new steel mills—fell away with his 1937 death, World War II, and the later changing populations of Gary. William Wirt demonstrated the insanities of the ongoing 21st century "great lockout in America's citizenship plants."

Why do schools primarily function from nine to three, five days a week, nine months a year? Gary, Indiana, illustrated a hundred years ago that current conventional schooling practices are obsolete. The Visionaries do need to war against Tradition!

WASTED MONEY

The innovative Gary programs were in place for thirty years, with lower costs and higher test scores than in comparable Indiana communities. Success was achieved without grant money from rich corporations. Visionary foundations cited in this book—Kettering, Danforth, Sage, Mott, Ford, Chrysler among others—later provided money to progressive communities for research, experimentation, innovation, evaluation, but not to raise test scores or impose mandated programs.

Conversely, recent money from Traditionalist foundations bent on being "saviors of schooling" has basically proven to be an ineffective treatment. Most efforts have failed to raise reading and math test scores through rigid mandated structures—especially among minority populations.

The May 9, 2011, *Newsweek* article "Back to School for the Billionaires" exposed the fallacies of the moneyed power foundations, none of whom know much about learning—only schooling. Written by Rita Beamish of the Center for Public Integrity, the documentation illustrates the features of the recent "education reform" measures. Over the past decade, Traditional foundations poured $4.4 billion into wrong solutions: Gates $3 billion, Walton $5.38 million, Broad $440 million, and Dell $400 million, augmented by others such as Kipp and Hewlett Packard. Even had they been successful, primarily only a few urban districts were served; where is such money for the other thousands of districts?

MONEY wasted for cognitive test score increases is not and never has been the answer for enhancing American education! Improvement is through affective personalized learning approaches imagined by Visionaries of the past and present, and for the future. Educational futurists state: "In a world of copycats, be an original."

> I am dejected over a society in which much of the population is addicted to technology, heavily indebted to huge corporations, and no longer interested in the classical achievements of the past.
> —Jules Verne

> Innovative educators are like orchestra leaders. They turn their backs on the crowd.
> —Everett Rodgers

Chapter Seven

Disturbing Priorities

It is in fact nothing short of a miracle that the modern methods of instruction have not entirely strangled the holy curiosity of inquiry; for this delicate little plant, aside from stimulation, stands mainly in need of freedom. Without this, it goes to wrack and ruin without fail.
—Albert Einstein

RETHINKING CURRICULUM

Curriculum organizational requirements in the current inane traditional 21st-century schooling formats need to be destroyed for the present, and certainly for the future. Visionary Army leaders understand this immediate priority. The Traditional Army politicians do not comprehend the rationale; they have made matters worse by insisting on further separation of learning categories.

Knowledge is interdependent; it is not segmented. There can be no separate "subject" periods in the secondary schools, "math class" hours at the elementary level, "departmentalization" in the universities, or specific course requirements at any level. Fields of learning are not only interrelated but interdependent. T. H. Huxley, among others, wrote of this understanding before 1900.

How can algebra be split from geometry, geometry from trigonometry, trig from calculus or statistics? Learners should not be taught mathematical concepts in isolation. The needed information should be merged as one as they progress. How can "math" be separated from the totality of a proposed project? When determining whether to build a bridge, awareness is required of the impact on the human and natural environments, economics, and aesthetics. Remaining solvent requires a balanced checkbook.

How can "beginning reading" be separated from mental, physical, emotional, and maturation factors, and later the ascending ladder involving literature, history, and everyday living? How can reading and math test scores be separated from character development? Schooling is desperately in need of change now! Learning is "oneness," not slices of a pie.

Teachers, parents, community members supporting the old isolated subjects and courses curriculum have been bamboozled by the Traditionalist Army members. The latter claim there is not enough money to fund "nonacademic" departments—even though finances were available until the testing insanity exploded. Politicians claim that emphasis must be placed on separate science, math, and reading classes to beat the Japanese—and other countries with high test scores—on the "important" academic content. The Visionary Army, to date, has not fought hard enough to prevent being further overrun by the elimination of the "nonacademic" fields.

FAULTY COMPREHENSION

Politicians and school people do not comprehend how the "forgotten subjects" can be retained and opened to new excitement for many learners through personalizing learning. Technology will eventually change even further the learning possibilities in the neglected areas. Regardless of the development of better support through teaching "machines," the human touch cannot be eliminated.

The home-based education movement was "good luck" for those who could participate in the important conventional separations: art, music, languages, industrial vocations, family studies, physical and business education, personalized technology, agriculture, camping, outdoor survival, nutrition, fitness—any topic of individual interest and importance. Each learner should be able to focus for hours or weeks in a field(s) of choice, no longer restricted to potentially one hour a day for one semester—the usual practice in conventional secondary schools, and even less time in the elementary years.

In the realities of yesterday, of all the "old" offerings considered as minimally important, the field of learning once labeled home economics remains *the most important subject in the curriculum for the present and future*. In the not-too-distant past, this "nonacademic" was commonly required of girls (no boys) in the seventh grade as one semester of cooking and one semester of sewing. Though these studies can still be of interest and value, this description is not what the Visionaries in this arena implemented—long before all the more "academic sounding" replacement names were adopted.

For the futurists, who said the basics in education and life were related to the affective domain, what could be of more value than the human aspects of home economics curriculum studies: child growth and development, parenting, human relations and interactions, self-image, health, safety, nutrition, environmental sustainability, democratic decision making, responsibility to self and the global village, and lifestyle priorities? Voluntary simplicity remains an important aspect of personal and global futures.

Of the Visionary programs under the old label of home economics, education of the whole person was, and still should be, a major
goal. Outstanding models excelled in interweaving the affective
and psychomotor domains with the cognitive. The nurturing of caring, warm persons and parents who could live in harmony with
themselves, nature, and societal conditions was a purpose that far
exceeded the need to graduate youth who received A report cards in
science, math, and English, but who did not have the characteristics
needed as neighbors, politicians, and corporate leaders. Objectives
included the promotion of equality, protection of the environment,
and the fostering of positive relationships.

MISGUIDED VALUES

Sadly the realm of "home economics"—whether conventional or
innovative—remained a second-class citizen. New legislation mandated more math and science studies, but not human relations.
"Home ec" was reduced in funding and finally eliminated in most
secondary schools. At the elementary level, where it should have
been a top priority, it was never considered by Traditionalists. Futuristic Visionaries created beautiful programs for young people,
but the conquering army finally eliminated these magnificent efforts which were overrun by political power.

Of what value is the ability of science to make an atomic bomb
if it is to be used to destroy people? Hiroshima was justified—in
defense, not attack—to save lives. Now will a hydrogen bomb
solve the global dilemmas? Does the answer lie in the affective
domain and the human values of the neglected "nonacademic"
home economics?

In considering the future for learners, the past does have many
lessons. There were probably no more unlikely 20th-century heroes
than Orville and Wilbur Wright, two bicycle-shop proprietors, who
without high school diplomas and spurred by the success of a mod-

el that at first flew only three and one-half seconds, revolutionized transportation, led to the Space Age, and changed the world. Should not politicians understand the need to capitalize on interests, aspirations, goals, and strengths for each individual?

The future of America lies not in more mandated "academic" requirements and higher test scores, but in personalizing learning for each Orville and Wilbur Wright. More teachers of the "sage on the stage" classroom variety are not the answer; needed are more pied pipers who can be "guides by the sides" for every learner. Such change can be and has been accomplished with no additional budget, but it does call for restructuring of conventional formats. To break the monopolies of Traditionalist schooling, the answer lies in more experimental three-second flights by learning Visionaries.

EXPANDED EXAMPLES

Thus far, the "old home economics" possibilities have been illustrated as one example of the wrong focus in eliminating forgotten priorities. Sought now are leaders with vision who can again create exciting learning venues for learners in all the neglected studies. Art, music, drama, foreign language—taught at the elementary level—the "old" industrial arts/technology programs, business and job-skill offerings, volunteering in the community, and school-age mothers programs, are just as important as science. Interdependent avenues are the keys for the majority, who are reached through their *strengths*, not their *weaknesses*.

What is wrong with providing focus programs for those interested in art, music, and drama? Immersed in creativity, they will learn more of the "old academics." When they do study interdependent—not isolated—curriculum options, they do so with willingness. They know there are some of the old "basics" they need and want to learn.

The college preparatory requirements mandated by traditional politicians have been a failure related to helping the young to love and to care for humans, animals, and the planet. Most of the huge industrial giants that are polluting the air and water and influencing legislation through political action committees with their money are run by educated but not always ethical people.

In the corporate world, engineers received A in science and math from outstanding academic campuses. The same is true for "name" campus graduates who are board-of-director members and who earlier received As in economics and political science. The corporation lawyers received As from the best law schools. *Is it not ironic that the supposedly best graduates from the best universities have created the greatest American and global problems?*

Should not "education" play a major role in addressing societal and ethical issues? Once again the question: are high test scores the answer for the future—or perhaps instead, should the focus emerge from the forgotten priorities eliminated or reduced by Traditionalists? Such learning concerns were highlighted by the thinking Visionaries!

> People learn best when they have a need to know. Learning is a deeply personal, affective experience involving self-concept. The genius of good teaching lies not in providing information, but in helping students discover needs to know they never had before.
> —Arthur Combs

NEW REALITIES

Interdependent curriculum and lifelong learning are not clichés, but already realities, as are the continuing electronic and biological revolutions, and the related brain-mind research. Globally, the world megafamines and megacities, the growing have–have not gap as populations increase, and the thousands of nuclear warheads are real.

Deforestation and desertification, mushrooming energy costs, global unemployment and underemployment, disappearing species of plants and animals, dangerous chemicals and drugs, toxic wastes, and air pollution contribute to the forgotten priorities of education. The rigor-oriented academic school people, pushing for a more basic common core curriculum, do not yet comprehend the urgent priorities for *Education* and *Society*.

High dropout rates, especially among American Hispanic, African, and native Indian youth, and the thousands of limited-English-speaking students further verify the irrelevance of current assessment tests. In many minority communities, 80 percent of these children may fall below "grade level" by grade three on state standardized evaluations.

Visionary leaders of the neglected "second class" education groupings need more risk takers who will fight the Traditionalist demands for a core, and insist on reinstating the fields of learning they represent in ordinary schools. There is a call to produce more research and development activities that could emerge, further supporting their claims of the value of "no required curriculum." Essential is more imagining and inventing; the minority must pioneer for the majority.

LABOR MARKET

The problem of the increasing numbers of working mothers does interrelate with curriculum issues of child growth and development, changing lifestyles, homes of the future, and cultural differences that interface with the priorities of curriculum. Economic systems correlate with the roles of the affective domain and the overwhelming burden created by emphasis only on the cognitive. Schooling has for decades equated school subjects with the workforce. But now there are probably over three million college graduates competing for former "blue collar" jobs.

The long-standing misguided politicians and corporations have responded by raising requirements: non-diploma jobs to diplomas, diplomas to degrees, degrees to higher degrees. Not everyone can be a computer analyst. Needed are greater numbers of such careers as custodians and restaurant workers, not computer programmers. Passing algebra does nothing for these job seekers.

Is it any wonder there is more youth crime from low-income neighborhoods? Those who live there see multimillion-dollar sports and entertainment contracts awarded for being tall and able to shoot a basketball, or sing with a rock band that happens to catch on with the fad of celebrity status. Can anyone justify the greed of corporate salaries, benefits, and bonuses?

While a few make millions and billions, societal conditions worsen as (1) more youth try to enter the labor market; (2) disadvantaged adults fall further below the poverty level; (3) relocated workers are unable to find jobs; and (4) older workers retire with insufficient income and health benefits. The percentage of lawyers to the total population is overwhelming. It is little wonder that the nation has been overrun by lawsuits and laws that provide legal loopholes for corporations.

Are all these—and more—national and global conditions related to nine-to-three school days, nine months a year? The Traditionalist Army says NO. The Visionary Army is fighting to make these many topics relevant in the curriculum. Learning opportunities need to be expanded, not restricted. For Visionaries in education, it is not hard to comprehend why it has been so wrong to reduce or eliminate the many "noncore" learning fields. This assault has occurred under the political control of school people. As so often stated, politicians know little of learning; they are only mechanical robots operating upon illogical assumptions.

For all the children some of the time, and for some of the children all of the time, the classroom resembles a cage from which there is no escape.
—Phillip Jackson

FALSE EXCUSES

The operative discussion is why did the forgotten priority "subjects" disappear entirely or suffer reduction—disappearance in most communities—without a whimper? The budget cuts are a false excuse. The extra time supposedly needed to increase the 3R curriculum has no research to support the value of more math rather than more home economics. If limited "academics" are so crucial for the future of learning, why did the Traditionalists allow Latin to disappear? It was once a "must take" required subject to enter name universities.

If Latin was dropped, why not also an archaic course called algebra? It was mandated not because it was essential for college, but as a political response to the pressure of preparing all students for "higher education"! For many years, mostly Caucasian college prep students took algebra. Those not planning on another four years for a degree took business or general math—classes not considered as meeting college-level preparation.

When minority populations began complaining that they were receiving a lesser education, the answer was easy. Require algebra of everyone; there could be no complaints! All would then have the opportunity to meet the demands of university admission. The fact that no one really needed algebra, the same as no one needed Latin, was never considered. However, it took the pressure off the controlling politicians.

Current education—compulsory schooling, compulsory learning—is a tyranny and a crime against the human mind and spirit. Let all those escape it who can—any way they can.

—John Holt

OVERCOMING TRADITION

Back to the future! Visionary leaders must force a reexamination of the concept called curriculum. The past traditional nonacademic fields—and new ones for the future—are as important as "academics." The fight must continue to overcome reductions of opportunities. Expanding the curriculum makes sense; narrowing the curriculum does not! Homework is a ridiculous concept.

Twentieth-century requirements are no longer valid related to "mandated course work." The Visionary Army must launch stronger attacks; ACTION is required to overcome tradition. No longer can there be "forgotten priorities." Related to solving the dilemmas facing education and the global society, all learning is equal in value. The "forgotten" Visionaries need to launch a major invasion against the tyrants. The 100 Years War Against Learning continues. Will visions ever overcome traditions?

> We, the State, have for a hundred years, gathered our children together in school from all classes of society, upon a common ground, for a common purpose, and then have rested our case for a democratic education upon the self-satisfied assumption that this democracy of intent is sufficient, even final. We have allowed it to presuppose a democracy applied, practiced, and produced! We must be rid of this vanity. An honest analysis will show that the school as a democratic institution has progressed no further than a decree of compulsory attendance.
> —Rita Sherman

The state, in formulating in the fullest detail, a syllabus which had to be followed in all subjects of instruction in all the schools . . . did nothing for teachers who ought to have tried

approaches themselves . . . but the yearly examination system controlled all methods . . . which was fatal to the true interests of education.
—Edmond Holmes

Chapter Eight

Choice Alternatives

Dear Pencil-Pal,
How do you go to school? I ride in a school bus. I go to a big
school. We learn a lot. They teach us science, English, geography, arithmetic, history, and spelling. When I get big, I would
like to drive a school bus.
—Charlie Brown

MY WAY

Flushing High rote taught me. School was a place where you
gave them back the facts they told you. School had nothing to do
with living, thinking, feeling. . . . What little education I received during my schooling years I owed more to public librar-
ies than to schools.

William Van Til, born in 1911—another reference of one hundred
years of war over the future of learning—wrote these words in his
1926 school-day remembrances. His CHOICE OF ALTERNA-
TIVES to traditional schooling was to spend as much time as possible in the former candy store building converted to a public library in the Flushing section of New York City. There he could
focus on his preferences, reading every book of interest.

In his school days, promotion and graduation were by semesters—not ended in most communities until circa 1948. He was moved ahead one semester four times in the elementary grades while attending P.S. 15. His junior high years at P.S. 92 were worse. The outcomes resulted in his often feeling as a social, physical—and in some subjects as math—academic misfit in high school. He was at least two or more years younger than most classmates. With no technology or other options, and with parent pressure for college, he felt trapped. These experiences are recorded in his autobiography, *My Way of Looking at It*.

Gifted as a reader, writer, and speaker, he later spent the influential years of his professional career in education doing his best to convince school people to overhaul existing notions of curriculum. He tried to "modernize"—to "futurize"—the focus from subject-oriented to student-oriented learning; he worked to have education move away from the disillusionments he experienced with the requirements imposed upon him during his mandated "school days."

LEADERSHIP YEARS

Throughout his thirty years of curriculum leadership, including a term as president of the national Association for Supervision and Curriculum Development (ASCD), Van Til tried to lead toward future learning environments by promoting concepts that for years had been rejected as "progressive education." He rigorously fought against the 1980s/1990s "reform movements," labeling those mandates as nothing but "more content and methods that had not previously worked well—more required courses, more credits for graduation, more remedial classes, and more."

Sadly he noted that such ill-conceived reforms that did not make sense were mistaken by the public as improvements! His views were repeated before his 1989 induction into the Ohio State University Education Hall of Fame—joining the legacies of the list of former Visionary education leaders at that then top-ranked institution.

Were Van Til still alive, there is no doubt that in analyzing the Traditionalist Army curriculum requirements, politically preached to the masses as solving the future and preparing students to cope with 2030 and beyond, he would have proclaimed the insanity of the Traditionalists. His opposition to the reforms of the 1980s and 1990s—for what were advocated for the future—emerged long before the advent of 21st-century technology. He strove, instead, to personalize curriculum.

Though supporting most of the innovative programs during the 1960 to 1980 era, he viewed new directions for curriculum within the existing schooling and university structures. He did not actively "don the famous white suit of armor" and lead the fight for Choices of Alternatives. He, and the boards of directors of the majority of the national education organizations, felt that perceived "radical" proposals, such as *Deschooling Society* (Illich 1971), would have difficulty gathering support from the masses.

As Visionary leaders, they failed to publicize in bold frameworks that they never proposed eliminating all Traditionalist Schooling. Unfortunately, they did not push hard enough for Democracy in Action by informing everyone, everywhere, that the "regular school" would still exist, but would be just one of many CHOICE ALTERNATIVES.

> The founding fathers in their wisdom decided that children were an unnatural strain on parents, so they provided jails called schools, equipped with tortures called education. School is where you go when your parents can't take you and industry can't take you.
> —John Updike

FLUSHING REVISITED

How does the past—the 1920s years at Flushing High and the ASCD Van Til–led curriculum reform efforts of the 1960s to 1980s—relate to the tasks required of learning Visionaries leading to the 2020s and beyond? The formats for change may be complex, but the responses to the questions posed are very simple. Global conditions have been rapidly changing. Traditional education cannot meet the challenges of the future.

The winter 2011 *Population Press* (Blue Planet United) documented clearly that the next twenty years will NOT be like the past twenty. The prophecies for the coming decades cited the evidence, not conjecture, for serious differences—and not just in technology. The NASA Goddard Institute for Space Studies determined that the 2010 global surface temperatures were the warmest on record; the 2000–2010 decade was the warmest since such records were first kept in 1880. The projection was that the 2010 statistics would not stand for long, as the expected warming trend would continue. The record-breaking snows, tornadoes, floods, cold temperatures, mudslides, heat waves, and fires that followed in the next months supported these expectations.

John Muir stated years ago—and before him writers stretching back to Henry Thoreau and even Jules Verne—that the narrow materialism of the emerging society was creating a deep alienation from the natural world. Supporting earlier views, the 2010–2011 United Nations Food and Agricultural Organization announced that the food price index was at an all-time high—and headed higher. Countries such as Ireland, Spain, and Greece were already basically bankrupt. What will the 2020–2025 global conditions reflect? What relationships, if any, do these climate, food, and economic conditions have with Traditional American Education? Will recent programs such as Race to the Top solve these future dilemmas?

The 1920s Flushing High and P.S. 15 / P.S. 92 Van Til experiences relate to the Goddard Institute statement that the next twenty years will not be like the past in every arena of society except the public schools. As Van Til would have noted, the Traditionalist schooling reforms of the 2010–2015 period will not benefit emerging societies.

Visionary Army leaders, given these ongoing but more pronounced 21st-century challenges of population, societal, and economic conditions, must be more determined than ever to unfold preferable educational futures. Can 2020 finally result in overcoming 1920 Flushing High education? To succeed in this hundred-year goal, the Visionary Army must prevail against resistance from the Traditionalist Army. How, within existing realities, do communities begin educational transitions toward 2030–2050? The ongoing response: only by confrontational ACTION.

BEGINNING TRANSITIONS

The near-term conflicts demand that the concept of Choices of Alternatives is finally sold. One option is for leaders to create a 2020 version of "Tomorrow's Schools," as envisioned in 1966 by President Johnson. That possibility is only ONE of at least thirty different selections that can be implemented within the same budgets as provided for current schooling. Each created option should be available to everyone. There is no "regular" or "deviant" program; there are no negative choices.

In implementing change, utilizing emerging technologies to the maximum will greatly assist; electronic support was not available in the 1920s and 1930s, or the 1960s through the 1980s. The fact that the IBM-created "Watson" could beat the best contestants on *Jeopardy* illustrates the potential. Watson was an exciting, fun invention. But Watson could not invent Watson! Maybe someday, but for now it takes human and personal touches to envision the next bold steps—the next "Tomorrows"!

As a student at Flushing High, William Van Til perceived what was wrong with the existing traditional schooling curriculum requirements and methods as early as the 1920s. As a director of ASCD, and with Hall of Fame leader J. Lloyd Trump of NASSP— and the many other Visionaries of the 1960s–1980s decades—all clearly described what was wrong with the hundred years of 20th-century schooling!

With the pen and with the tongue, these Visionaries tried to reinvent education. They illustrated better ways to organize course work, create new structure formats, and improve the evaluation of learner progress. Lloyd Trump illustrated one way with his "Trump Plan"—later described in his *A School for Everyone* (1977). Such insightful innovators of the various national education organizations in the 1960s–1980s era influenced hundreds of other Visionaries. However, with only the pen, they were unable to mobilize strong enough opposition to force the Traditionalist Army to retreat!

The problem, upon reflection, was obvious. These organizations were national in scope. Stanley Elam, the outstanding editor of the *Phi Delta Kappan* journal, editor Tom Koerner of the *NASSP Bulletin*, and editor Ron Brandt of ASCD all published success stories. Great educators such as John Goodlad and Robert Anderson and deans of innovative university programs such as Dwight Allen at University of Massachusetts—all were eventually squashed. The controlling Traditionalist school people and politicians won again.

The 30-percent Visionaries were so excited with the 1960s and 1970s successes, that they assumed the 40 percent middle-of-the-roaders would eventually support new directions, thereby overwhelming the 30-percent extremely rigid resistors. As in politics, the latter campaigned so hard that they convinced the moderates to "not change so fast"—thus maintaining a 51 to 60 percent control of the old system of schooling.

MASS SOLUTIONS

The professional organizations try to represent the "masses." ASCD, NASSP, NAEP, and AASA, among others, in spite of Visionary leadership during the Golden Age of educational change— the 1960s and 1970s—had to represent everyone eligible to join— from right-wing conservative school people to very liberal left-wingers—along with the moderates in the middle. "Educators" of any political persuasion could join and be elected to the governing boards.

It has been difficult to have these national organizations fight with vigor against Congress for compromises that would support multiple divergent choices. The result has been their inability to take a strong stand against regressive political swings. They try to present a variety of views, and try to represent the best learning environments for everyone, but because they cannot commit to forceful ACTION, the erroneous one-size-fits-all political mandates remain in place. Even with the best leaders and concerns for all learners, these groups have allowed learning injustices.

TRAGEDIES CONTINUE

American Indian youth between ages fifteen and twenty-four are committing suicide at a rate three times the national average. Unrelenting poverty on most reservations fuels the problems. In South Dakota on the Pine Ridge Lakota Sioux Reservation, the largest and poorest in the state (and perhaps the nation) the rate of suicide is ten times the national average—as is also true on the Lower Brule and Crow Creek Reservations. Suicide is the second leading cause of death among American Indian youth.

The K–4 age reservation children do fine in school as far as traditional "academics"—especially in sites where American Indian cultures and arts are prominent; the children are smart! As the grade levels advance, they learn their ancestors were drunken savages who massacred the whites. Only recently have they begun to learn that the commanders of the cavalries and generals, such as Custer, were wrong; the cavalry massacred peaceful Indian tribes, including five hundred women and children at Sand Creek, Colorado.

Later, science classes at Pine Ridge had "ditto sheets" enabling the students to count the legs on crustaceans. Why, when they had never seen the sea or even a lake? On the Choctaw Reservation in Mississippi, students copied on a blank map of the fifty states, the state capitals of each, which were clearly provided for them on another sheet. Why? Indian education under the Bureau of Indian Affairs (BIA) was a disaster. The same was true when control was transferred to the local districts. The only modicum of success was achieved by the tribes that were able to direct their own schools.

NASSP, during the reform movements of the 1960s–1980s, had an Indian Exchange Program involving six innovative public schools and six Indian sites to try to help improve reservation school conditions, especially in those directed by the BIA. American Indian "schooling" disasters were known then, but Congress let the sadness continue. The Indian youth suicide figures quoted were not 1960, but 2010. Education organizations had no power to force—but only suggest—choices of learning alternatives for these youth. The reservation children were perfect examples of "Every Child Left Behind." This legislation counted these youth as just numbers in the NCLB math and reading statistics.

The reservation schools were not provided with enough resources, though at the same time corporation executives and "celebrities" were allowed to amass fortunes. In May 2010, Meg Whitman, former corporate CEO, spent $150 million of her own corporate-earned money plus the Republican war chest—to try to defeat Jerry Brown in California for a $200,000-a-year job. Why? For greed of corporate political power and control—as with traditional mandates to continue faulty schooling practices.

Not only are Indian youth neglected, but so too are thousands of poverty-level children and families representing all ethnic groups throughout the fifty states. The millions of dollars poured into Title I federal programs to help overcome these conditions were well-intentioned, but seldom administered correctly by states and school districts; the results were few long-term significant differences in their "schooling" test scores. Why, and how, are candidates for the coming presidential elections allowed to collect billions by charging thirty-five thousand dollars a plate at a fundraiser dinner, while thousands of Americans starve on the Native American reservations?

> School is a war against the poor.
> —The Schoolboys of Barbiana

PAST MISTAKES

Yes, this is the 21st century. The focus of this book remains the future! Can Visionaries realistically overcome the many cited Traditionalist controls and instead insist on choices of learning styles, alternatives, and programs for each individual? Certainly—even in lean budget years. Philosophy and structure, not money, can create many nontraditional options that Traditionalists commonly reject. One simple example illustrated previously is a nongraded team of "guides-by-the-sides" with multiple spaces and ages of learners, versus the all-in-one-room format directed by "sages-on-the-stages" for a given chronological age. The cost is the same!

The big mistake made by the innovators of the most recent "golden age" for education (1960–1980), was trying to create programs that would fit everyone. The open classroom schools were great for those teachers, parents, and students who understood the concept and volunteered. But for those Traditionalists forced away from "my room" and into an open-space building, the results were disastrous. Under a Visionary school board, superintendent, and principal, the flexible Walker Elementary site in the Amphitheater District of Tucson, Arizona, was the most exciting program in the country. The parents who requested were allowed to transfer to a nearby "regular" school.

When the Traditionalists regained control of the school board, they fired the superintendent and principal, put money and walls into remodeling the building, and forced Visionary parents to attend that neighborhood school. Choice was not understood. Those who loved the original Walker had no place to transfer. The leaders of the accompanying pioneering Canyon del Oro secondary school then left. This K–12 Arizona model was vanquished.

The Visionaries of those days failed to cement long-term conversions of choice. Approaching 2020, the politicians and school people are only viewing the future with traditional tinted glasses— not with reflections of the "Golden Age." They understand "their one way," failing to acknowledge efforts to offer choices of learning environments. Charter schools, and some home-based education programs, are ill-designed offerings controlled by the Traditionalists to give the impression that they are open-minded. Most districts and states have ruined the initial dreams for charters.

Politicians now are more demanding for the majority, insisting on additional "academic requirements." They maintain rigid grade-level divisions—dividing students into elementary, middle, and high school facilities—while strengthening separate course mandates in the continuous efforts to "beat the Japanese" and the rising test scores of the Chinese. For the Traditionalist Army, the PAST is still the FUTURE! For students, the 2000 decade was worse than that of 1950. Visionary 2020 leaders need to "squash" misguided efforts of 1990–2010 forcing everyone into the same mold. The controllers of yesterday have never accepted choices of alternatives on a national level.

WHY NOT

To succeed, current Visionaries should offer optional—not mandated—learning choices for the future. The ten thousand members of the Progressive Education Association worked hard to change schooling to learning during their four decades of leadership, circa 1900–1940. They were involved in the *Eight-Year Study*—comprehensive educational research. Ralph Tyler, a future Hall of Famer and foremost educational researcher, was hired to ensure trustworthy evaluation. He was also a long-time leader of the *National Society for the Study of Education*. In 1993, shortly before his death, he reviewed his 1902–1994 life span and seventy years of focusing on improving education.

Upon reflection, Tyler stated: "Learning takes place better when the plan for it is in harmony with the way children learn. . . . There could be no such thing as a standard curriculum for everyone. . . . Restructuring curriculum as called for in the Nation at Risk report was absurd." He further noted that "the problem with the high school curriculum was that it was built on what subjects people thought students ought to have rather than what the kids needed."

Powerful earlier groups and leaders as the Progressive Education Association and the National Society for the Study of Education could not cement choices of alternatives for the FUTURE! The 2020 Visionaries, with all existing knowledge, further research, and exploding technologies, can overcome the Traditionalists of the past one hundred years. Finally, schooling can become learning. All that is needed is that clarion to heed a national call for AC-TION—for Visionaries to demand change at the state and national levels!

Why has it been so hard to create learning choices for everyone? One way to learn how to shape the 2020s and 2030s is to continue to review past realities. Insightful knowledge from Detroit can be used to end the domination of the Traditionalist Army. The future of the Visionary Army resides in unifying all who wish to escape traditional schooling.

FASCINATING EXPERIMENT

The story recounted by now-deceased Morrel Clute, former national curriculum leader and professor at Wayne State (Michigan) University, is a perfect example of the need to escape schooling for most learners. The results proved that the controlling Traditionalists did not understand learning, but the involved Visionaries only used the PEN; they were not able to defeat the enemies. The outcome documents that it is long past time for the SWORD.

Nonconforming teenagers from inner-city locations in Detroit, who had failed in passing their classes, were given a chance to advance to their next school level in the fall if they did well in a special summer program at Wayne State. Transportation and meals were provided for those who finally agreed to attend. The first day the staff asked those enrolled what they wanted to learn. These youth were smart; no one responded. The silence continued for three days, as they were not going to volunteer for "schooling assignments." Finally, after much boredom and restlessness, a student challenged the staff. "We want to learn more about sex."

The communication line was open. What and why did they want to study this topic? The responses were strong and clear. "We live in neighborhoods with drug pushers, pimps, prostitutes, vice." Soon a personalized flexible curriculum was in full swing as they engaged in such core topics as sociology, psychology, health, home economics, science, politics, citizenship, and law enforcement related to the theme.

They did math and statistics regarding costs, English for audio interviews and written journals, art through painting street scenes, and world history through tracing prostitution and crime. They listened to many volunteer speakers—sociologists, psychologists, health officials, vice-squad members. It was a wonderful display of interdependent curriculum relevant to the student. Most received As and Bs; all were promoted to the next level.

The Traditionalists in the Detroit schools did not learn. Upon return, these students were placed in the usual style of classes—period 1 math, period 2 English, period 3 world history. Most began to reject such irrelevancy, received poor grades, became discipline problems, and eventually dropped out of high school. The Detroit system would not employ a former Peace Corps worker who had spent two years in Africa, had a degree in geography, and got along well with these students as a summer grad intern. He had not taken the course "Methods of Teaching Social Studies in the Secondary Schools"; they claimed he was not eligible. If ever a case study proved the need for choices, this Wayne State experience left little doubt.

21ST CENTURY

Efforts to provide choices have not succeeded in the first two decades of the 21st century! The charter school concept started with great hope in 1991; however, overall results have been negative related to the original dreams. Not one of the fifty states has yet to grasp a handle on how to achieve significant success. The laws governing charter school approval are so convoluted and different—and are not even needed. In most states, local school boards have the authority to grant flexible choices without such legislation. In California, the state superintendent was given the authority to waive every requirement in the Education Code except for earthquake safety.

So much paperwork is required that in many communities the concept remains silent. Charter approvals have been used for low-achieving students or for ethnic minorities to create schools reflecting their culture—both with the wrong intent. A few have provided ways to avoid required open enrollment membership through field trips, teacher aides, and in-home learning. There have been those not honest with their use of funding.

The majority of charters are too small, have inadequate facilities, do not offer sports or exciting music programs, and face enrollment limitations via lotteries and transportation difficulties. Few have been truly visionary; most follow their state curriculum mandates. Seymour Sarason, professor at Syracuse University, predicted these problems in his 1998 book, *Charter Schools: Another Flawed Educational Reform.*

One example of the abuse of charter school statistics is the acclaim given to high-achieving programs. In the Los Angeles school system, the top scorers on state tests were charter schools. The district opposed the original approvals, for they pulled money from the general funds that must be allocated to each site based upon enrollment. On closer inspection, the achieving charters were mostly in high economic college-prep neighborhoods—a way to separate the "upper class."

Seldom are model charters in the various states in low economic minority neighborhoods. Arizona law requires instruction in five core subjects; it falsely equates *instruction* with *education.* The freedom to create entirely new learning systems is lost for most approved charters. The ill-conceived concepts need to be completely revisited and given new licenses for learning for the many—not just old schooling for the few!

GREAT BOOKS

Why is there in the 2010–2020 decade the need for another book deploring what has existed for over a hundred years as "education"? Why is an increase in a war against tradition necessary? In the 1960–1980 improvement efforts, great books by learned scholars and critics were gold mines of why and how schooling could change. The negative among the prevailing optimism was revealed by one question: "Will current schooling ever be replaced by more humane, happy, democratic forms of learning?" The good news was—yes! The bad news was—NOT in this lifetime.

During this most recent Golden Age of hope, Edward Blishen wrote: "Schools usually have one thing in common—they are all institutions of today run on the principles of yesterday." In *Pedagogy of the Oppressed*, Paulo Friere wrote that education was suffering from "narration sickness" (teachers speak; students listen). Paul Goodman in *Compulsory Mis-Education* wrote that "schooling is no longer designed for a changing world . . . with its increasing set curriculum, stricter grading, incredible testing; it is a vast machine to force acceptable responses. . . . To educate, we must get rid of Compulsory Schooling."

In *How Children Fail*, John Holt wrote: "We destroy their enthusiasm for learning by the intense, competitive nature of schooling—replete with grades, gold stars, and days filled with dull, repetitive tasks." Concurrently, Ivan Illich in *Deschooling Society* wrote that "for most people the right to learn is curtailed by the obligation to attend school." In *Education and Ecstasy*, George Leonard wrote: "Schooling is a terrible thing to impose on kids. It is cruel, unnatural, and unnecessary. . . . Schools as they are now are designed to produce unhappiness." Carl Rogers in *Freedom to Learn*, noted that "schools constitute the most traditional, conservative, rigid, bureaucratic—and in our time—the institution most resistant to change."

The Golden Age era published many more of these great books. Dozens of authors could be cited. One of the best summaries of the period is an outstanding work, *Toxic Schooling: How Schools Became Worse*, by Clive Harber. With all the intellectual power and agreement by so many Visionaries, why and how did the Traditionalists maintain control? They were able to mute the voices of parents, teachers, students, writers, and major conferences on change in education. How did they survive the criticisms? It was the failure of the Visionaries to ACT—with cannons, not pens! In this innovative period, their proposals and programs made so much sense that it was just assumed that education was headed toward "Tomorrow's Schools"!

There was a lack of recognition of the abilities of the resurgent Traditionalists not only to maintain the hold they had, but to eliminate the pockets of hope in all fifty states. The most recent phase of the 100 Years War has been ongoing for four centuries. Now it is well into the fifth—labeled the 21st century. Is there any hope for a different future for learning? Will there ever be alternatives for all learners to pursue freedom of choice for their own education?

> To learn to know oneself and to find a life worth living and work worth doing is problem and challenge enough, without having to waste time on fake and unworthy challenges of school—pleasing the teacher, staying out of trouble, fitting in with the gang, being popular, doing what everyone else does.
> —John Holt

> I wrote that schooling can seriously damage your education, but I was too cautious. I should have said, schooling will damage your education.
> —Roland Meighan

Chapter Nine

Exemplary Possibilities

The language of reform carries with it the traditional connotations of things gone wrong that need to be corrected, as with delinquent boys or girls incarcerated in reform schools. . . . School renewal is a much different game—the ethos of renewal has to do with people—and improving their learning environments.
—John Goodlad

BLACK MOUNTAIN

Traditionalists have difficulty in envisioning extreme deviations from the old conventional university and K–12 schooling structures; most even reject minor modifications. However, for the Visionaries who do IMAGINEER, the rainbows are filled with dreams of realities that could be—and should be—in existence now. Somehow the Traditionalists see as necessary the usual classrooms of science, English, and math, with the current and coming technology making the classes more rewarding.

For those who are capable of imagining, one exciting example from the past, using "higher education" as a catalyst, proves the potentials of the future. This break with tradition occurred at Black

Mountain College, located on six hundred acres of the Blue Ridge Mountains in North Carolina. Black Mountain was a challenging learning experiment in education. It could easily be replicated for the 2020s, and be even more unique in its possibilities.

University campuses are familiar with the college-within-a-university structure. With so many of the state universities bulging at the seams and overwhelmed by the size of the enrollments, the smallness of a Black Mountain experience would be welcomed by numbers of faculty and students; further, the concept can be replicated at no additional cost. Black Mountain was private, but the same philosophy can be applied to a publicly supported setting.

Founder John Rice believed tradition-bound education imprisoned potential; classrooms were a poor atmosphere for learning and living. Though in existence only from 1933 to 1956, Black Mountain was a magnet for artistic and academic pioneers; it featured a form of freedom encouraging designs for new ideas and concepts. Centered on the arts and creativity, with a focus on the individual, the students were enveloped in an intense self-directed education for living, learning, and creating.

Black Mountain was a school of rebels that recruited more rebels. Here Buckminster Fuller designed his first geodesic dome. Joseph Albers advanced his color theory. Robert Harshenberg made paintings with shadows, John Cage composed music with silence, and Merce Cunningham began to revolutionize modern dance. This search for freedom attracted a group of radical educators and numerous European dissidents. Students lived in rural mountain conditions, but they formed an unparalleled community of learners. Two books, one by Martin Duberman and the other by Mary Harris, describe how a unique philosophy functioned in a nontraditional environment.

SMALL STEPS

Today and especially tomorrow, such thinkers are essential to help address the even greater global dilemmas than those that existed during the Depression and World War II years, both of which contributed to the inability of Black Mountain to survive. However, it is easy to perceive such freedom existing in the 21st-century public domain. If another John Rice would emerge, the purchase of a small rural college in financial difficulty, a former dude ranch, an older resort, or a struggling golf course could provide the rural Blue Ridge openness for a private institution.

In the city public sectors, the college-within-a-university would work well, especially—though not necessary—near the edge of the campus where some dormitory and classroom spaces were already in place. At the high school level, a wing or floor of the building could be set aside as far from the central traditional spaces as possible. All students could and would intermingle throughout the campus.

The philosophy is able to emerge with greater strength when not handicapped by being placed near excessive traditions. The middle school can follow the same wing or floor arrangement. If a small elementary school, then "down at the end of the hall" space could become a Black Mountain environment for self-directed learning and creating for those who volunteered.

Black Mountain had only minimal technology: Ma Bell telephones, electricity, knowledge from the construction factories, and music and art from the "old masters." But it had the inventive spirit of Thomas Edison, and the amazing long-range projections of Jules Verne. Imagine the Black Mountain capabilities armed with the electronics revolutions of the 21st century. This ninety-year old dream from the past has been featured only to illustrate that there are so many Exemplary Possibilities for the future of learning if only Visionaries will finally overthrow the stranglehold of the Traditionalists and loosen a barrage of learners to Imagineer the future for living, learning, and creating.

RETRENCHMENT DECADES

The retrenchments in educational politics of the first two decades of the 21st century requires transitional steps to reach freedom from "schooling" for those who volunteer. The task will be easier as the years pass, with growing resentment, poor results with the test, test, test mentality, and expanding use of technology. Educators of the second half of the 20th century did not know to use early computer advances. Period 2 algebra of thirty students in one room with a sage-on-the-stage continued as the norm.

Fortunately, there were many Exemplary Possibilities that did emerge. The innovations can be used again—after being eliminated once in many communities. Already with virtual schools, *instant* worldwide visual and audio communications and online learning, new patterns merge with past creativity to force schooling toward learning. Hard-to-believe changes during the coming two decades will be accepted. If Visionaries arrange environments where they can "start from scratch," the horizons are limitless. If they must begin with small steps against Traditionalists—even as with guerrilla warfare in some locations—the key is to *start*.

Schooling is finished when one looks ahead; learning is just beginning to reemerge. New Black Mountain environments where freedom is alive can provide the beacon toward the future. Schooling has never been necessary; learning is a viable goal. Briefing books on how to get "educated" despite school confirm that the current education systems are causes of harm for many pupils and teachers. *Damage Limitation: Trying to Reduce the Harm Schools*

Do to Children by Roland Meighan provides solid evidence that the Army of Visionaries must take strong ACTION against the army of ill-informed politicians and conformist school people.

BACKWARD STEPS

Technologically oriented Visionaries are in demand. It is certain that "machines" are going to change the mechanical world—an expanded communication rather than an industrial revolution. However, if past is prologue, Traditionalist technologists are going to try to "fix" schooling futures. They are not the thinkers needed; the hope is that those with Vision can create the "unimaginable dreams" of years past.

Few who grew up watching "the man in the moon" foresaw the possibilities of visiting "him" one day. In the past three retrenchment decades, the Traditionalists have done their best *not* to "visit the educational moon," but to prevent the possibility. In the opening half of the 20th century, sites such as the University of Chicago and Ohio State University were acknowledged as educational leaders.

In the closing half of the 20th century, Dwight Allen, as dean at the University of Massachusetts, created the most innovative, flexible graduate program in the country. There, legitimate, scholarly PhD degrees were available in a very individualized fashion; concentrations in educational futures, educational alternatives, futures curriculum, and organizational patterns were among the dissertation topics. People came from throughout the country to a place called Amherst.

What happened? Traditionalists of the educational regression years forced Dr. Allen out of office; the entire creative, innovative program was returned to a traditional graduate school format with limited choices and many structured requirements. The stories of what befell great nontraditional K–12 and college options could fill a book. Why did the Visionaries allow these programs to be eliminated by a flood of unopposed political pressures? There was only a slight whimper of protest.

Innovative nonscheduled secondary schools abandoned period 1-2-3 schedules; these are prepared by people in the spring who have not even met the new students who enroll in the fall. Alarmed by schedule reforms, music department instructors in most school districts protested loudly to school boards. Accompanied by traditional music-oriented parents, they demanded a return to one hour of orchestra, one hour of band, and one hour of chorus, as a minimum. Most community boards caved in to the pressure to retain, or revert to, Traditional scheduling.

The few innovative open-ended schools that survived created exciting better-than-ever music programs. One model used was the Lawrence Welk method. That rhythm style did not have to be reflected, but the interrelationships of the instrument groups remained. Welk used every instrument found in orchestras and bands, some additional ones not commonly involved, and singing and dancing diversities. The combined "Welk-style" groups could play any music desired with any arrangement.

All members of the total ensemble did not have to meet every day for one hour. Smaller groups could meet as needed—whether the strings or the brass, or a chorus combination. When preparing for a concert or an all-school musical, they could come together through the daily flexibility of nonscheduled curriculum hours. The results were astounding, but Traditional school people, under political pressure, returned to the old concepts; the "new" innovations were lost.

Linus: I wish I had a pencil-pal like you, Charlie Brown.
Charlie: Well, it doesn't do much good if you can't read or write
Linus: That's very true—only five years old and already I'm an illiterate.

We move around the same endless circle of Band-Aid reforms. We have agreed on a major resuscitation effort, with promises to breathe life into an exhausted national school system. The systemic problems will continue untreated. American schools will remain in crisis. Where can we begin with an effective treatment?

—Lloyd Elliott

RECAPTURING TOMORROW

Online colleges, virtual schooling, and other forms of emerging technology will serve a small percentage of learners until "education" can be completely transformed. The great majority of learners yet will be engaged in forms of schooling—until more Visionaries heed the call for learning. For now, working parents will want partial-day child care, and the socializing factor of the few better schools. Unions will want older youth kept out of the labor market. The police will not want large numbers roaming the streets. Most parents will be in the mold of "send the child to school to learn to read."

For the near term, these reasons are all valid. The problem is that overwhelming numbers of youth will not be in transformed schools or other worthy alternatives. They will be forced to stay in traditional neighborhood schools. The answer for now is to ensure that choices of learning environments are provided for all students, parents, and teachers. The mechanics are easy; the politics are hard. The reality is that so much is at stake—including the present and future lives of millions of youth—that Congress, state legislatures, communities, and schools must allow the creation of equal options for everyone.

Of the thirty easily identifiable designs—proven and effective— ten are briefly described to help Visionaries illustrate to parents the choices that can become available. With support, Visionaries can force the Traditionalists to offer personalized options for children. Ironically, if a family has three children, each of them could, not surprisingly, select different options. The goal is to personalize learning, not to push everyone into another version of a same-size-fits-all structure. The offering of only one or two options to "regular schooling" is not enough. Visionaries must campaign for individual choices for everyone.

TEN DESIGNS

These ten identified designs are not the ultimate, and certainly do not reflect what might be available in 2030. They are plans that can be implemented immediately with existing budgets, staffs, students, and facilities. No one of the ten is "better" than any other. These are not competitive "we are the best" solutions. They are only realistic remedies for beginning to break the lockstep stranglehold of current schooling politics. These all can be blueprinted in detail, as each has been used successfully.

The patterns can be adjusted related to the size of the district: huge Los Angeles, California; midsized Spokane, Washington; small Springfield, Vermont; or rural Waubey, South Dakota. There are almost no districts that cannot create several options related to learning choice styles. Teachers in one-room schools of forty students of mixed ages have used concepts of choice: example, the British infant school. Size, budget, and transportation are not valid excuses for implementing only one variation as an "alternative school." All families should have the opportunity to move out of traditional schooling patterns.

1. *Total School Design:* In two, five, ten, twenty schools, depending upon district enrollments, individual sites can receive waivers of regulations from their own board and superintendent, or through appeal to the state education department

or the legislature. They can be allowed to create unique non-traditional learning programs for the future. Many schools have used this model in the past. Among the most famous were the now-closed (by "backroom" politics) Mankato Wilson Campus School at Minnesota State University (MSU); the St. Paul, Minnesota, Open School (continuing but restricted—again by politics); and private school models such as those at Sudbury, Massachusetts, or Albany, New York. Remember that the thirty schools in the landmark Eight-Year Study deviated on an individual basis from traditional rituals.

2. *Cluster School Concept:* The Southeast Alternatives project in Minneapolis created choices of four *cluster* rather than *neighborhood* schools: an open environment, a nongraded format, a free school, or a traditional program. Parents, students, and teachers selected whichever one fit their philosophy.

3. *Two Schools-in-a-School:* Two choices—one the traditional schooling model and one a creative new learning model—can be housed within one building; competition as to which is better is not permitted.

4. *Three Schools-in-a-School:* Three completely different philosophies—traditional, semitraditional, or personalized—can exist well in one building, related to different concepts of the best for each learner. (See the summary page describing Garden Lake Middle School, where the Lincoln, Jefferson, and Washington models illustrate fifty program diversities.)

5. *Four Schools-in-a-School:* As an example of use in a large high school, this design is easy to describe. Six hundred students each in four completely different learning philosophies can exist beautifully with the flexibility of sharing expensive swimming pools or the one Russian teacher. One wing is traditional, one is semitraditional, one is a futuristic Black Mountain, and one is a series of "academies," including a

language immersion program and perhaps a school-in-the-community. Students from all four can play on the same large conference football team, or the four can form their own teams and play in smaller enrollment conferences.

6. *Multi-Available British Infant School Models:* An optional plan designed for K–12 (or college) youth, not just restricted to the originally conceived K–2 years, where forty kindergarten, first-, and second-year students shared learning stations. Mixed ages teach each other and progress in learning as they individually develop.

7. *Integrated Elementary/Middle/High School/College:* Students of all ages are mixed in designs that allow the creation of unique individualized patterns that do not copy traditional school separations. There could be one or many such facilities in a district, each free to follow its own model of learning for the future—the key being the freedom to deviate from separated elementary, middle, high school, and college designations. Under one roof there is just one learning center.

8. *Research and Development Center(s):* No existing structure. Planned to be the NASA experimental programs for the district—free to design and implement visionary but realistic demonstration models to reach the moon. The Space Centers are to create 21st-century learning—not schooling.

9. *Modernized Versions of the Plans for the Once Futuristic Learning System for the Proposed Minnesota Experimental City:* The MXC was to have no schools in the community, only project centers to use when desired. Everyone was a "teacher"; everyone was a "learner." Age did not matter. Learning connections were made via the computer or by recommendation.

10. *Varieties of Charter Schools:* Freed from local school board–approved restrictions, a district may encourage parents to invent designs that meet the concepts of the original

dreams for charter learning centers. Volunteers are not handicapped by varieties of schooling; they are granted freedom to
invent the future—with the only caveats related to segrega-
tion, health, and safety factors. Those who wish can create
full programs utilizing former schooling facilities that allow
full-blown sports, music, arts, home, business, industrial concentrations, physical education, and technological futures.
The small, restricted charters of two hundred may be viable
for many families, but size and facilities should not interfere
with desired learning systems for the next decades.

These designs are realistic; they can be described in detail. Many
have been portrayed in the book *Educational Alternatives for Everyone* (International Association for Learning Alternatives). The
purpose of outlining these ten suggestions is not to tell people how,
but to encourage Visionaries to imagine, invent, and implement
new designs. They become the Wright Brothers and Sisters who
can create educational opportunities. The constantly repeated goal
is to insist that the Visionary Army members rise in unison and
force the Traditionalist Army resisters to relinquish their political
control, to allow patterns to unfold for the coming decades.

GARDEN LAKE

To those in doubt of the reality of options, one model of a three-
schools-in-one middle school is presented. The following fifty
characteristics describe the possible differences among three programs in one facility. Picture a building with three wings, or three
floors, or other spaces to separate, as well as possible different
student choices (portable classrooms)—acknowledging use of common facilities as in gymnasiums; however, they offer completely
different philosophies.

In this model, Lincoln is the free, open, futuristic learning center of five hundred students who can, with staff and parents, imagine entirely nontraditional patterns. Jefferson, another five hundred students, is a modified program—partially stepping away from traditional schooling patterns. Washington, with five hundred youths, maintains a structured schooling format. Garden Lake was originally built for fifteen hundred; there is no additional cost to the district. Yet staff, students, and parents have the freedom to select whichever of the three learning frameworks fits them at this moment in history. Alternatives are promoted; this table offers concrete realities of choices for most everyone.

GARDEN LAKE MIDDLE SCHOOL

Lincoln Learning Center	Jefferson Learning Center	Washington Learning Center
Overlapped, nongraded, 5th–9th	6th, 7th nongraded; 8th graded	6th, 7th, 8th grade levels
Student scheduled, daily	Modular schedule: 1-2-3, MTWTF	Conventional periods
Individualized instruction	Continuous progress instruction	Teacher-directed instruction
Self-selected studies	Modified requirements	Required classes
Interdependent curriculum	Integrated curriculum	Departmentalized curriculum
Students select facilitators	Students have teachers assigned	Students select from teams
Students select advisors	Students assigned to advisors	Students assigned to counselors

Goal sheets/ portfolios—no ABCs	Only ABC+ no credit—no D–F	A B C D F grades
No homework; long-range projects	Weekly assignments	Daily homework
Personalized YRE calendar	60/20 YRE calendar	Nine-month calendar
No textbooks	Reference-only textbooks	Textbooks assigned
Rooms modified as suites	Rooms adjacent	Rooms by grade level and subject
Tables, flex furniture, some carpet	Some tables, some desks, some carpet	Desks arranged for custodians
Affective, psychomotor, cognitive	Cognitive, affective modified	Cognitive is priority
Food service all day	Lunch within block of time	Assigned lunch period
Optional attendance any 180 days	Required track attendance	Required daily attendance
Flexible hours 7 a.m.–5 p.m.	Some early/late flexibility	Required hours for everyone
School in the community	Some time in the community	Mostly in the building
Differentiated staffing	Modified staffing	Traditional staffing
Nonacademics are equals	Academics and electives	Academics featured
Designed on student success	Designed on success/ failure	Designed on student failure
Self-paced learning	Accelerated learning	Grade-level learning

Teachers as facilitators	Teachers as initiators	Teachers as presenters
Students are responsible	Students partially responsible	Teachers are responsible
Experimental school	Partly experimental	Nonexperimental school
Community center	Limited community center	School center only
Self-satisfaction outcome	Occasional rewards	Rewards and punishments
Five-phase methodology	Modified group methods	Whole-class methods
Personalized programs	Partially personalized	Mandated programs
Facilitators work in teams	Teacher-team cooperation	Teachers work in isolation
Open-ended curriculum	Flexible curriculum	Required curriculum
Technology individualized	Technology modified	Technology group-paced
Environmental illness focus	Environmental illness concern	Environmental illness doubted
Community volunteering priority	Limited school volunteering	After-school volunteering
Open enrollment	Modified enrollment	Designated enrollment
No waiting lists	Modified lotteries	Waiting lists and lotteries
Evaluation as R&D project	Some R&D projects	Exemplary standard model

Early childhood personalized	Flexible early childhood	Standardized early childhood
No eligibility rules	Modified eligibility	Standardized eligibility rules
Human relations priority	Human relations considered	Human relations mandated
Dress as appropriate	Flexible dress code	School uniforms
Concept oriented	Concepts and content	Content oriented
Brain-based learning	Brain research aware	Traditional courses
1-1 conferences key	Student 1-1 often	1-1 for problems
Humaneness first	Humaneness considered	Rules first
Individual diagnosis	Small-group diagnosis	Large-group diagnosis
Perception as priority	Perception awareness	Standardized perception
Intelligence research applied	Intelligence by judgment	Intelligence by test
Decentralized budget	Partial budget control	Total budget control
Cultural exchange travel	Possible cultural exchange	Conventional classes

Chapter Ten

Preferable Futures

The future is ours for us to create. But creation requires knowledge, imagination, and perseverance. Will we generate these qualities in sufficient measures to change the world? If we fail, more destruction is certain. If we should succeed, none of us has sufficient imagination to perceive the potentials of our future.
—Robert Theobald

THOUGHTFUL CONSEQUENCES

Writers who consider themselves futurists often refer to the forty possible global futures, twelve of which are most probable, but only three of which are considered most preferable. Futurists never predict or even project specifics. They instead write based upon their interpretations of the data and events available for reflection at a given moment in history. On the gloomy side of one or more of the ± forty possible futures is an all-out, worldwide nuclear war. Hydrogen bombs could almost provide an outcome for humans similar to that which befell dinosaurs.

On the sunny side of one of the ± three envisioned preferable futures is the potential to end all wars, eliminate global poverty, and preserve sustainable clean air, water, and food for all of humankind—and the animal kingdom too! For only 10 percent of the money spent worldwide on the arms races, hunger could be abolished among people in every country.

The majority of futures writers yet interpret somewhere along the ± continuum from among the twelve most probable. They do not foresee global suicide, but neither are they very confident in the ability of humans to overcome the search by many for greed, power, and control. The cognitive, corporate, political, and corruption worlds win against the goals of global affective futures. The victories of the latter are usually short-term gains achieved during accidental moments of human and natural tragedies.

Worldwide, countries suffer from nature. That is a reality that will continue. The past decade has witnessed earthquake disasters in Japan, Haiti, New Zealand, Chile, Indonesia, Pakistan, and more—natural fires, volcanic eruptions, unusual flooding patterns, mudslides, hurricanes, tornadoes, and tsunamis. The question that must be addressed: has every possible stone been turned in the effort to minimize such global tragedies? What are school children learning regarding the future of the world?

There is no denying that knowledge of math and physics to build dams, roads, aircraft carriers, airplanes, and computers is still essential. Analytical study of history is required to rethink whether World War II could have been prevented. The construction trades need skilled architects and builders to design essential service buildings such as safe-as-possible hospitals.

Technological advances and sciences are mandated for research on cancer, the control of pollution, and wind energy. Such lists, including the potential elimination of printed books, could take an entire chapter. There is a need for traditional knowledge and innovative advances in all fields; the issue is how these are learner concerns for present and future generations.

Traditionalist politicians—unopposed by school people—continue to see the need for required former "engineering math classes"—algebra, geometry, trig, calculus—taught with the same methods that cause huge numbers of school dropouts. These "courses" do nothing to address poverty, population, war, crime, pollution, or energy consumption. The compilation of human concerns is part of the endless list that Traditionalists assume will be addressed better with online technology.

Visionary learning leaders and societal critics perceive the need for learners to have options for what they personally need and want to know through personalized choices—not mandated classes. Cannot the lessons of the past help create—at least in education—a better future?

> I do not care to motivate my children by telling them that they will have to be strong to survive ruthless competition. I would rather tell them the world needs their wisdom, their talents, and their kindness—and of the many possibilities for a life of service.
> —Nat Needle

DISASTER PREVENTION

Natural disasters cannot yet be prevented. However, most human-related causes can be minimized. The annual floods in the United States serve as an example. Initially the political planning commissions that approve building in floodplains are often involved with the developers. There is no excuse for such grants in 2020. In the early continental history, most villages and then cities were built along rivers—understandable then for transportation or agriculture—and on small plateaus among mountainous terrain. In spite of fiscal concerns, corrections can be made now to past mistakes—or at the time—essential priorities.

Communities can declare eminent domain and force people to move out of flood zones. They can build higher levees and higher, stronger cement flood walls. Where possible they can divert the river channel around population centers. People can build on high, solid blocks to let most water pass under without damage to the structures. A combination of such potential corrections could reduce many human tragedies while lowering insurance costs.

These moves would not guarantee 100 percent protection, as unexpected rare "monsoon rains" from nature might overcome all human efforts. However, there is no excuse for not preventing many human-controlled disasters. The control of flooding, in conjunction with excessive rain and snow, requires political will to find resources, revise building codes, and arrange for people to be better protected. If individuals refuse to move—"this is my land"—then the community should be less concerned and helpful. It is nice to live alongside a stream and enjoy its beauty, but not if it floods homes two out of three years during spring runoffs.

CHANGING HISTORY

"Everyone" has long been aware of the many worldwide changes that have already arrived and those on the near-term horizon. The retirement of the historic Discovery shuttle—taking its place in the Smithsonian alongside the Wright Brothers version of flight, the Spirit of St. Louis, and the famous military planes housed there—is only a tip-of-the-iceberg reminder that history is in flux. The enormous possibilities for the coming space exploration can perhaps help lead to one or more of the envisioned preferable futures.

Not only are the technological aspects for the decades ahead cause for reexamination of concepts, but more important is the need to reexamine the concepts involved in societal systems. The brilliant, but admittedly controversial, Albert Einstein addressed social reforms and the potential contribution of education many years ago.

Einstein was always opposed to capitalism—which he saw as an "evil system." He eloquently described both a more humane society, as well as a caring education system. He joined Albert Schweitzer and Bertrand Russell lobbying to stop nuclear testing, and with the controversial Paul Robeson, cochaired the American Crusade to End Lynching organization. In a 1949 issue of the *Monthly Review*, he wrote: "The education of individuals, in addition to the promotion of innate abilities, must attempt to develop in each person a sense of responsibility for humans in place of the glorification of power and success in the present society."

EDUCATOR VIEWS

When views of possible futures are presented to the Traditionalist Army leaders, they see many of the same concerns as do the futurists. However, most respond that the best way to address the societal needs related to education formats is to continue the same in 2020 as in 2000—but with improved implementation and better teachers. The same curriculum will be required to ensure higher test scores in reading, math, and science—aided by the yet advancing technological inventions.

Traditionalists say that society will always need engineers, scientific inventors, foreign relations experts, skilled military directors and equipment, and linguists who can decode enemy messages. Therefore, they reason that what is now taught, and how it is taught, with tweaks to update conditions, should continue for the coming decades. They believe that just doing better what is being done now will advance world-class preparation toward the future.

When members of the Visionary Army acknowledge the same potential possible futures, they also see advances in technology aiding learning. Contrary to the Traditionalists, they cannot comprehend how in any way "schooling" as it now exists can remain.

They ask again: Will world-class test scores in math lead to the elimination of poverty in the United States—let alone in the global villages?

Will high test scores end pollution, corruption, and provide for a sustainable society? Visionaries see these affective societal crises as forcing the necessity for interdependent learning—not continuing with separate schooling subjects. Current curriculum should witness the merger of such as biology, physics, and chemistry into one learning field. Visionary leaders do not comprehend how anyone could disagree to end Traditional rituals.

One reason is clear why *Declaring War Against Schooling* is so adamant that Visionaries must engage in a real war, speak out, and refuse to obey many of the awful laws passed by politicians. It is a call for a civil rights campaign for learning. Cesar Chavez fought for migrant workers. The demands relate to one of the statements by Martin Luther King Jr., who said: "There comes a time when silence is betrayal."

Visionaries have reached the betrayal stage via their lack of concerted ACTION—the awakening of Congress! They have written so much; the included bibliography documents only a handful of the over three hundred books that could be cited. The writers have used a bold pen; they have yet to mount the cannon. Because of such delays, more than ever is there a call for an "atomic bomb style" attack.

Learners cannot be sacrificed, hoping that schooling traditions might slowly evolve. The Visionaries continue to fail in grabbing the attention of the Traditionalist politicians and school people. To work toward preferable futures, the absence of the "bomb" in education has been a "silence of betrayal." It is essential that Visionaries end that silence. Do educators want one of the thirty-seven other possible futures, or do they want a learning society, one of the three preferable visions? Once again is that call for Direct Action—immediately!

DISCONTINUITY REALITIES

For preferable futures, it is important to foresee possible discontinuities. Ironically, there were eleven unforeseen happenings that destroyed an otherwise perfect plan for the Japanese attack on Midway in 1942 and caused their defeat. There was another great lesson related to the 2011 earthquake and tsunami in Japan. As the world turns, if such a monstrous national stroke of bad luck had occurred in Japan in the 1943–1945 period, most citizens in the United States would have cheered, as they did the death of Osama bin Laden in 2011. The horrible enemy got what it deserved; Pearl Harbor was avenged.

In the second 21st-century decade, the "hated" Japanese are now an important ally of the United States. Further, those born after 1945—now seniors of sixty to seventy—or young elementary age children were not part of the 1940s attacks on the countries of the Pacific Rim. Times change. Hopefully the Japanese culture has changed enough that the aggressive expansion they tried in the 1930s and 1940s is no longer among their goals. The people of Japan needed help in 2011; deservedly, much was provided. Witnessed was the dignified response among the Japanese people: the absence of looting, the caring for community—a societal virtue—helping each other survive.

The disaster in Japan—overall such a highly educated country—could have been much worse. They were probably the best-prepared nation in the world to withstand a 9.0-magnitude earthquake. They had built many "earthquake-safe" buildings and had maintained the third highest world economy behind the United States and China. They were among the global experts in developing "safe" nuclear power plants. Their leaders assumed they were relatively immune from such 2011 dramatic acts of nature.

Two mistakes were made—related to the concept of discontinuities. The Japanese built too near a major fault line; seacoast towns were allowed to develop almost on the water. Within three miles of the coast, entire towns disappeared. Four miles from the coast, most survived the horrid tsunami—except those built in narrow ravines where the water converged and soared upward.

Yes, Japan is overpopulated for its geography; space is at a premium. To their credit, they did build "quake proof" buildings (they thought), but construction in a potential tsunami zone might better have been limited to necessary port facilities, not residences. The 2011 tsunami was never expected. They also acted on projected "hundred-year safe" quake and flood projections. There is no way to prevent such calamities. What if the San Andreas Fault in California were to receive now a 9.0 quake? What would happen in that state, with the ensuing ripple effects across the nation? The 1906, 1933, 1980s–1990s quakes there—in contrast—would be mere blips on the hundred-year timetables.

Related to education—the disaster in Japan being only illustrative of uncontrollable natural phenomena and human-caused global tragedies—should not the past cognitive priorities be shifted to be shared with the affective priorities and people concerns? Cannot the learner focus first on the prevention of poverty, hunger, ensuring safe living quarters, and the struggle for positive sustainable environments? One hundred years from now, people may have gone the way of the dinosaurs, or many may be living in such seemingly potential outposts from Earth as perhaps another planet. But for the present, what are the priority concerns?

Once more—and again, and again—will higher test scores overcome wars? Can more be done to prevent the extreme negatives of natural and people-caused floods, fires, hurricanes, tornadoes, earthquakes, and the remaining list of calamities? To continue the "twelve probable futures"—more of what the world is now—then schooling will and maybe should remain as it exists. If there is a deep inner conviction to move toward more preferable global futures, then schooling must transform to learning.

The United States cannot control the action in all 195 countries of the United Nations, but it can change locally, and do all in its power to create a greater focus on thinking globally. One example is taking the lead for moving worldwide towards learning—with the potential spin-offs on societal conditions. This seemingly impossible order may be just a vision—a figment of imagination—but the possible is no longer working.

GROWING OBJECTIONS

During The 100 Years War against learning, both writers and doers have been trying to focus communities away from traditional schooling toward personalization. The 1960s to 1980s era witnessed exciting changes, innovations, experimentations, research studies, and implementations of sensible ideas. But again, politics won. The passage of Proposition 13 by tax benefactors in California destroyed one of the best education programs in the nation. The election of President Reagan shortly after completed the demise. State after state reverted as Traditional school people let similar parents gain control of the school boards.

In 1995, California had over two hundred districts offering exciting twelve-month Year Round Education (YRE) learning programs. In 2010, only a handful remained on a reduced scale. Most states that had year-round continuous learning programs abolished most efforts. Why? YRE makes sense. Politicians destroyed it. Minnesota, the leading state for innovation, retrenched most all excitement except for a few active charter schools and Area Learning Centers (ALCs) that have survived. The Visionaries were defeated; the Traditionalists gained and maintained a win/lose philosophy of control over a nation bent on "schooling."

One can review, again, educational history to learn of the current seeds of discontent. On August 26, 1937, New York City Commissioner of Parks Robert Moses wrote (paraphrased here) in the *Herald Tribune* that the play areas under the control of the Board of Education were built at great cost to meet the needs of immediate neighborhoods. Closing them, unless expensively supervised, is wrong; the areas should be part of the inalienable rights of children to play in safe public places. A major purpose of education is to give children healthy opportunities for the development of their bodies in proper surroundings. The notions of the Board for excessive control over the passive areas of the play spaces are "just plain bunk."

Into the fourth decade since President Reagan, the frustration with cognitive schooling has continued. Though controversial for years, the opposition to the No Child Left Behind law—passed, of course, by politicians—is finally reaching ACTION crescendo! Still in the "pen" rather than the "marching" stage, there is again hope.

COLORADO DOWNHILL

Angela Engel, in *Seeds of Tomorrow*, has provided a fresh look from the view of a younger mother and former teacher. A few years earlier, Emmanuel Bernstein, a senior citizen and author of *Secret Revolution: A Psychologist's Adventures in Education,* described the same concerns. All the many "new writings" by Visionaries in the 21st century only document further the pleas for learning, not schooling; they join the dozens of profound writers of the 20th century.

The cause for the recent Engel comments relates to the awful CSAP tests—the Colorado School Assessment Program—similar to most current Traditionalist-imposed state school testing programs. Ironically, in the "Golden Years," Colorado was a leader in innovation.

Invented there was the unique Concept 6 year-round education plan. Denver was headquarters for Designing Education for the Future—the Eight Rocky Mountain States Project. The Cherry Creek, Aurora, schools were nationally recognized, with visitors from all fifty states. What happened? Yes, once more, politics! The CSAP requirements symbolize what is wrong with state assessment plans in all the states that adopted "world-class testing" as the evaluation tool for successful schooling!

During the 1960s–1970s period in Colorado, additional exciting programs emerged: the Jefferson County Open School, the Tanglewood middle school alternative, and the Evergreen alternative led by Arne Langberg. The Colorado State Department had an innovation unit headed by Eugene Howard, the nationally recognized leader and former superintendent and creator of the pioneering Ridgewood High School in Chicago.

The *Changing Times Journal* was published by one of the two best-choice organizations for learning options in America—the Colorado Alternative Education Association. This group joined with the Minnesota Association, advocating for diversity in educational opportunities. The CADRE national group for educational innovation, also in Denver, was supported by the visionary Kettering Foundation of Ohio. There was the flexible K–12 program at Idaho Springs.

The futures-oriented traveling International Graduate School of Education (IGSE) was also headquartered in Denver. The author of this book was the keynote speaker for the Colorado School Administrators Conference on Educational Change, and for the University of Colorado (Boulder) Conference on Alternatives. He was the banquet speaker at the University-sponsored Harl Douglass lecture, the last one attended by Dr. Douglass before his death. Colorado went from positive "leadership" for better forms of education to negative "followership" for retrenchment in schools—all because of Traditional politicians.

Recently the Employers Perspective study, "Youth Being Ready to Work," identified the skills needed for successful careers. They were professionalism, teamwork, oral communication, ethics, and social responsibility. These are not skills measured in Colorado by the CSAP, or the federal No Child Left Behind law.

The Engel commentary emphasized that the CSAP would not improve the education of a child. To the contrary, the negative is that high-stakes testing produces stress, anxiety, and excessive competition. Assessments as the Colorado one-size measurement cannot be trusted to indicate items of confidence, cooperation, and compassion; they certainly do not evaluate student achievement, teacher effectiveness, and school quality. Income—not talent—correlates highest with success on these rigid tests.

Especially handicapped—evaluation data confirm—are the number of children on free or reduced-price lunch, students with disabilities, second-language learners, and those from low-income families. Yet with negative outcomes, Colorado has spent $50 million a year developing, administering, grading, and summarizing test scores. The only possible use of the results is for diagnosing individual growth in a relaxed personal environment. They are never of value for group comparisons; they are wasted money during a period of budget crises.

TEACHER EDUCATION

It has long been recognized by the Visionaries that teacher education programs, offered in excess by college Traditionalists, have been a major stumbling block in changing from schooling to learning. The credential system has not created the best chance for a preferable rather than a possible future. Summarizing why is easy. As a child, the eventual candidate is enrolled in a lockstep graded classroom with one teacher in a square box facility with limited possibilities; seldom are they given the opportunity of enrolling in a team-taught, non-graded personalized learning system.

The traditional junior high—renamed middle school—adds to the indoctrination. The seventh grade is the worst abomination in schooling history. No one should suffer its indignities. Then on to four years of high school period 1-2-3 classes and requirements, report cards, tests; the only relief is found in a few electives and cocurricular activities. After these thirteen years of brainwashing, they attend a traditional university teacher program. Required courses are taught by professors who had suffered through the same system; they teach the potential teachers how to "teach" the way they were taught—not to help children learn. It is a vicious recycling system that reproduces clones of the clones.

Nontraditional college instructors are few. Those who survive are often denied tenure, or if accepted, are not esteemed by the majority of the faculty. The teacher education majors are not exposed to alternate ways. No wonder the creative persons leave the "profession." The career longevity of good teachers equates to most running backs in the National Football League; the majority last only five years. The individual beginning teacher must fit the structure to retain a job. As persons with needed income, they cannot buck the system of schooling.

Unions have failed to help create diverse learning systems. They have reinforced the accepted ways, feeling that conforming to what exists is the best way to continue demands for salary increases, shorter hours, and smaller classes—none of which improve learning or add to the chance for preferable futures for learners. Unions were a necessity when educators had to bargain individually for their salaries, and administrators and staff could be fired on a whim by a new board or superintendent.

Unions could break the lockstep schooling system of today; statewide and nationally, they need to refuse to accept bad legislation, or at least fight to the bitter end with politicians. Instead they have seldom uttered a whimper except when related to teacher—not learner—creature comforts, as in salaries and working conditions. Many unions, representing a "profession," have often not demanded professional dress codes; some "teachers" appear in old dungarees, sneakers, and T-shirts. It is well known that most considered "professionals"—physicians, engineers, lawyers—have higher "test scores" than teachers.

PIED PIPERS

The goal is for teachers—as guides-by-the-side, not sages-on-the-stage—to help lead toward preferable futures. If colleges would change from the old system of "general ed" classes as a frosh, "observation" as a sophomore, "participation" as a junior, and "student teaching" as a senior, guides-by-the-side could help the change to learning. What is needed is to identify "Pied Pipers" immediately. These are candidates who truly love "kids," who are recognized by the learners through "osmosis," and thus are loved in return.

First-year involvement with K–12 youth can determine the pied pipers. Those who are not can change their plans for a major, rather than waiting to take "Methods of Teaching Reading" courses. The "Pipers" should intern for a year, learning to guide by guiding. This takes school faculties who will move away from self-contained classrooms, work as teams, personalize learning for everyone, remove unnecessary requirements such as algebra, let students read when they are ready, and make learning fun.

Unions can create these changes. They can force colleges to change teacher preparation. They can force state Teacher Credential Commissions to eliminate all the overlap of requirements. Those who are Pied Pipers can "teach" any age level or any subject. They contribute their strengths and seek help from others for their weaknesses. If they are not Pipers, they do not belong in the profession.

PERSONALIZED SCHOOLS

In schools that have personalized learning environments, students have had great success. A girl who is a potential mother, but who is not planning on college, while in high school can enroll in university home economics classes. She may earn the equivalent of two years of college credits, with A/B report cards. Her self-esteem is raised dramatically, learning is fun, and the eventual families benefit tremendously. This story is drawn from a true example.

A boy who hates school—mostly because he wants to be an artist—but whose dad is forcing him to join the family architecture business—can be "saved" by allowing him to paint all year: murals on school walls, student portraits, assisting the art guide. No longer a discipline problem, he learns to like school, and eventually is successful as a "graduate," an artist, and may join his dad as an architect. This also is a true story.

Traditional schools do not allow such deviations from the required structure; they do not comprehend personalizing. Visionaries can ensure freedom of choice for the learner. Preferable futures are possibilities—not "pipe dreams"—when the affective domain has priority over the cognitive!

For physical development—whether for nonathlete or athlete— the psychomotor domain is crucial, especially for young children. The hero worship, money, and scandals involving those currently in colleges and professional leagues—and some in high schools—

must be addressed. Kindergarten psychomotor growth is more important than developing a star quarterback. Should school money be for quarterbacks or for kindergarteners? What are the priorities? There are politicians who can help create preferable societal and global futures.

GROUP ACTION

Are such changes possible? Yes, but again, it takes group action—as outlined in the potentials for teacher unions and administrator organizations. The Goodlad and Anderson publication *Non-graded Elementary Schools* in 1959 documented the fallacies of graded classrooms and reinforced many of the practices and advantages of the old one-room schoolhouse. But nationally schools did not "nongrade."

Therefore, in issue 13, 2010–2011, of the *Journal of Personalized Education Now*, Chris Shute wrote a fine article titled "Maturation—A Problem for School Based Education." It repeated, with up-to-date analysis, what Goodlad and Anderson wrote, and confirmed that the great non-graded schools of the 1960s–1980s period were superior to what exists today. Yet via politics, except for a few charter and alternatives schools programs, probably 98 percent of all youth remain in grade-level classrooms. Why?

Traditionalist army members may think that inventions—going beyond such simple current wi-fi, scrapbook-capable digital cameras, and some colleges going all green—no books or papers, just online capabilities—will eventually solve current educational issues. Perhaps innovations will; if not, they certainly can help. But in the second decade of the 21st century, most middle school-aged children are still locked in tradition. The only "improvements" may be technological additions.

A book could be written on what is wrong with that often referenced terrible seventh grade, on the research behind such accusations, and on designs for correcting requirements, curriculum, and school structure. The programs for the "middle seventh" are completely out-of-sync with the interests, needs, and philosophies related to the approximate student ages of ten to fourteen (if "grades" 5–8) or eleven to fifteen (if "grades" 6–8).

POTENTIAL HOPE

In the past two decades, Visionaries have recognized the failure of significant school improvement. Traditionalists prefer not to change; they hope that existing schools will get better. Recently, billions have been spent on reform and teacher training, but the results have ended with the same schools and the continuing headlines regarding the crises in education. There is an increasing demand for a revolution in public education. The existing system will not change itself, but change is urgent.

Donald McCabe of Rutgers University, in a 2001 study, demonstrated that cheating is an adult-created societal problem. Of high school students in conventional programs, 74 percent had cheated or plagiarized during the prior year. He concluded that students cannot be blamed in most situations when they are faced with impossible time-limit projects, observe continued corporate fraud, see parents skim on their income taxes, and know that many college athletes seldom attend class.

A learning system eliminates these problems. A schooling system compounds them. The author rid cheating from his schools through personalizing curriculum, even though he himself had "cheated" to pass several illogical group-paced courses in high school and college.

There is an overwhelming recurrent theme: the Visionary Army must rise and force the Traditional Army into concessions. This is where unions can be a positive force. The Visionaries need leadership and support from teachers. A few colleges have tried to change teacher education programs—Goddard, Evergreen State, University of North Dakota, Mankato State, Antioch, Nova, St. Scholastica, Webster, University of Massachusetts—but in the long run, all have failed. It takes a "global village" to create preferable futures!

Perhaps the classic *Peanuts* (Charles Schulz) again provides the rationale for hope for the Visionaries. Sally tells the story of her experience with the assignment for every classmate to create a coat-hanger sculpture!

> "A 'C'? I got a 'C' on my coat hanger sculpture? How could anyone get a 'C' for a coat hanger sculpture?"
> She asks the teacher: "Was I judged on the piece of sculpture itself? If so, is it not true that only years of time can judge a piece of art?
> "Or was I judged on my talent? If so, is it right that I be judged on a part of my genetics over which I have no control?
> "If I was judged on my effort, then I was judged unfairly, for I tried as hard as I could.
> "Was I judged on what I learned about the project? If so then you, my teacher, should also be judged on your ability to transmit knowledge. Are you willing to share my 'C'?
> "Perhaps I was judged on the quality of the coat hanger out of which my creation was made—also unfair. Am I to be judged on the quality of the coat hangers used by the dry cleaning establishment which returned my clothes on this hanger? Is that not the responsibility of my parents? Should they not share my 'C'?"

To create preferable societal and educational futures, perhaps the advice of Mark Twain remains appropriate: "Why not go out on a limb—for that is where the fruit can be found." Or more recently,

Ron Miller wrote that "education holism is a vision of healing. It is a vision of atonement between humanity and nature. It is a vision of peace. It is a vision of love."

Humane, heartfelt, personalized, and lifelong learning paths can help create a new future for humankind.

> The whole theory of modern education is radically unsound. Fortunately, in England at any rate, education provides no effect whatsoever.
> —Oscar Wilde

Chapter Eleven

Political Challenges

A general state education is a mere contrivance for moulding people to be exactly like one another, and the mould in which it casts them is that which pleases the dominant power in the government, whether this be a monarchy, an aristocracy, or a majority of the existing generation.
—John Stuart Mill

NEGATIVE DECISIONS

If all the negatives that have been presented against the majority of politicians in *Declaring War Against Schooling* were not reality, there would be no need for another volume documenting a call for ACTION. Unfortunately, the accusations are accurate; educational Visionaries are presented with an urgent responsibility to overcome the stranglehold of the one-view Traditionalists.

Conventional thinking has stymied every potential breakthrough in the past forty years toward learning systems for tomorrow. Traditionalists instead have moved toward schooling systems for yesterday. Sadly, the Visionaries have not seriously unified against the prevailing wind, except—as so often noted—with a proven, ineffective pen.

Politicians, national and state, during the Reagan, Bush, Clinton, Bush, and Obama years have passed bushels of hard-to-believe regressive education codes. Among them are the infamous national testing requirements, supposedly to solve the problems of schooling, and political competitions such as the Race to the Top solution, state tests for graduation, and backward curriculum edicts. Where were the Visionary educators?

Early in these decrees, some states even created tests for promotion in the lower grades. Georgia developed an unconscionable test for second graders that had to be passed before the children could enter the third grade. Several districts imposed required summer school for the "slow youngsters," intent on having them pass for their schools to appear successful. It is hard to believe that professional Georgia school organizations did not revolt; instead, most even supported this vicious schooling act. Later numerous administrators in the state were accused of erasing wrong answers and replacing them with correct responses, thus inflating fraudulent test scores.

Visionaries, though outnumbered, did protest these required insanities; K–3 children do not need standardized tests! However, Congress and most state legislatures would not even reconsider that their "reform legislation" would place education further along on the famous Bridge to Nowhere.

Serious testing and subject requirements should have received greater consideration for present and future schoolchildren. Reminders of important possible negative effects emerged worldwide. The very well-educated Japanese built in villages along the north coast what they thought were earthquake-safe buildings, strong thirty-foot high seawalls, and nearby nuclear plants. They failed to look ahead and ask—what if? In this case, the "what if" was a powerful sixty-foot tsunami that killed hundreds of schoolchildren and destroyed "safe towns"; nature overwhelmed the protective seawalls.

The politicians in the British Parliament did not look ahead and ask "what if" when in 1988 they passed the infamous Tory Education Act. They were intent on silencing the movement toward personalized learning systems in the United Kingdom. The lessons provided in the 1913 book *The Tragedy of Education*, written for England, were not even reviewed.

In the past hundred years, what have world politicians accomplished in poverty-stricken locales? What have they done for forced—not chosen—homelessness, or to assist the thousands of foster children? There are more than wars and profits for consideration; instead the priorities should be related to the possible effects of legislation on people and society. Enter, then, the important need for *learning*—not *schooling*. Political lack of insight and support, along with restrictive legislative acts, have created havoc for the societal microproblem labeled EDUCATION.

GREEN LIGHTS

Return to the Lone Ranger and his efforts "in the days of yesteryear" to improve conditions. In education, there was a Lone Ranger time in the not-too-distant past, when legislators and educators worked together to change schooling to learning. Rather than red lights stopping innovation, legislatures gave green lights to dream the impossible dreams. There were open-minded people who envisioned a new era toward personalizing education.

What happened to these leaders? Where are they and their young apprentices now? Those Visionaries who are considered by their supporters as "good" politicians and educators have become hopelessly outnumbered by the "bad." These latter individuals perhaps were well-intentioned when elected, but their success in being on the winning side saddled them with blinders. Potential political "learning advocates," and even Pied Piper school people fell prey to the nonsensical cliché of the "will of the people." Fifty-one percent to forty-nine percent—51 to 49 votes—is not a will of the people!

Even if one side won handily in votes related to education—perhaps 70 to 30 percent—what consideration has been given to the 30 percent losers? Is there not room for humane, nontraditional educational choices for the "defeated thirty"?

TRUE ARROGANCE

A revealing example of the 51–49 mentality occurred in a place called Chico, California. For fifteen years, five elementary schools had conducted fairly conventional but good year-round education programs. The teachers, parents, students were happy; a family could transfer to a nine-month school if desired (options in education). The approving school board politicians never fully understood the year-round concept philosophically, for parents in other elementary schools and in the junior and senior high schools were denied the option of YRE; however, the board allowed the five sites to proceed.

In 2006, a conservative majority (51-49) had control of the school board. They hired a Traditionalist superintendent who arrogantly insisted that to "improve test scores," all schools had to be on the same schedule. He declared he was ending year-round education programs.

Protesting parents, teachers, and students of the five involved schools waited too long to seek help from a knowledgeable consultant. When they did, they gathered five hundred names on a petition to retain YRE. The night when they were to present their petition and ask for reconsideration, the board decided not to put a discussion of YRE on the agenda. They would not accept the petition, or provide time for audience participation and discussion.

The board voted that all schools would return to a rigid traditional schedule. Even though the consultant outlined how the five schools could appeal for reversal, the faculties decided not to invite the wrath of the new board and superintendent. There were no leaders, no true Visionaries willing to battle the Traditionalist administration. The five schools surrendered. The Chico district teacher union refused to help. Teachers at the five schools were union members and wanted to retain year-round, but had no support from their organization, as the issue did not involve benefits.

The defeated accepted this "will-of-the-people" decision with hardly a sign of the now famous "whimper of opposition." Though not willing to defend year-round teachers, the union negotiated expensive coaching pay. In the "old days," coaches received no extra pay or a small stipend; they coached for the love of athletics and of the students on their teams. Such political, woeful, "one-size-fits-all" controls occurred throughout the nation; the Traditionalists had "won."

POLITICIAN SEARCH

From examples like Chico, it is clear that the plea for humane politicians must be intensified. Over the years, not all elected officials have been arrogant and regressive. There have been good people: open-minded, personable, and truly seeking the best for learners. For comparison to the negative 21st -century lawmakers, in the 1960s and 1970s Walter Mondale, Hubert Humphrey, and George McGovern were forward-looking senators. Not all supporters replacing schooling with learning were Democrats; many Republicans voted with them.

As politicians, these leaders advocated exploration; Congress was convinced to provide federal money for innovation and research to determine how best to move toward personalized learning. The majority of legislators then were not focused on higher test scores; their concern was finding paths to help each student not only with the basics, but with their passions and dreams. These Visionary leaders did exist. They agreed with the many societal critics on the need for a "new" format for education.

At the state levels, the positive 1960s/1970s legislators in later negative Colorado allowed and supported the leadership efforts to move education away from tradition. The eight Rocky Mountain states involved in the Design for Educational Futures included conservative legislators as in Idaho and Wyoming—elected as Republicans. It was not just "liberal Democrats" who perceived the need for new directions.

In Minnesota, which ultimately took the national lead for change at the state level, innovative educators were eventually supported by important conservatives such as Rod Searle, chair of the Senate Education Committee. Minnesota was the first state to authorize charter schools.

South Dakota had the best Title III projects/programs in the nation—again approved by Republican legislators and a Republican state Commissioner of Education; the changes were not for improved test scores, but for research and experimentation. South Dakota State University and the University of North Dakota—never previously bastions of liberalism—provided higher education leadership for future possibilities. They changed teacher education programs.

In California, the author was asked by State Senator John Dunlap to write a bill to promote educational alternatives. Education Codes 58500, 58502, 58507, 58509, and 58512 resulted, passed by both houses of the legislature, signed by the governor, and supported by the state Department of Education. It was clear that this 1976 legislation was approved to allow and promote choices of learning styles, endorsed by the legal codes of the state. In the same era, the legislature approved a seven-year research project for the Hayward, California, school district to experiment with a two hundred–day, year-round learning calendar.

Wealthy individuals were supportive too. Glen Taylor, eventual owner of the Minnesota Timberwolves, sent his daughters to the most innovative public school in America. Similar individuals were bolstered in their support by private national foundations: Kettering, Ford, Chrysler, Danforth, Mott. Their directors understood the urgency for fundamental new designs. There were both Republicans and Democrats who encouraged research, innovation, and experimentation.

The many humane elected leaders who underwrote optional choices for everyone were testaments that politicians can be "good guys and gals"! A major SEARCH now is required to uncover new educational Visionary political leaders for the 2020s/2030s era. They can help identify other politicians who are willing to turn the tide away from the "bad education politics" of the 2010s and again promote personalized learning.

It was not only the 1960s/1970s politicians who encouraged experimentation. In the 1900–1920s era, political leaders permitted John Dewey, William Wirt, Carleton Washburne, and Helen Parkhurst to pioneer new approaches. In the 1930s, the Eight-Year Study—which involved public-supported schools—was allowed to proceed. The research received help from the private Carnegie Corporation.

Test scores and "beat the Germans" school competitions were not the focus, although accountability certainly was a prime concern. The education faculties at Ohio State University, and Visionary educators as Ralph Tyler, William Kirkpatrick, George Counts, Harl Douglass, did not permit experimentation without evaluation. The difference from 1930 to almost 2030 is that a hundred years past, many politicians, parents, and benefactors not only allowed, but encouraged major deviations from conventional educational practices and rituals—in the effort to "meet the needs of each individual"!

POLITICAL MISTAKES

Current Traditionalist politicians argue that they are seeking better ways to improve schooling: passing Race to the Top financial grants for high test scores, promoting elimination of teacher tenure, firing ineffective teachers, increasing accountability, closing low-performing schools, destroying the power of unions and collective bargaining, mandating rigorous tests, using sophisticated technology, and requiring additional demanding curriculum.

Arne Duncan, secretary of education, in 2011 called for more arts. Yes, arts are important, but it was a sham call—for the administration emphasis was on math and science test scores—not "art tests." The word "arts" was used only to enlist support from the generally more fortunate parents with money and talent—parents who had been "trained" in the arts by their parents—to support Race to the Top concepts.

What else helps students? Ask younger men working in stores like Home Depot and Lowes. When one was told that wood, electric, auto, and welding shops were available in most schools earlier in the 20th century—and most male students were required to take wood and electric—he commented: "Wow, I wish I could have gone to a school like that." The Traditionalists have eliminated all those important opportunities. Arne Duncan did not call for more "shops."

The famous Wilson Campus School in Minnesota offered fun and career classes as choices. A feature was just "shop"—not broken into wood, electric, auto, or plumbing. All the possible subheadings were bunched as just one; the learner could pursue any of the "hands-on" shop arenas of personal interest.

Visitors to Wilson were stunned to see a group of older students—boys and girls—in "dirty clothes" in "shop" building a small, livable house. When the learners were asked about their future—are they preparing to be carpenters?—the response was no. Most were going to major in engineering. They were A students in math.

Their reason for shop, for as many hours or days a week as desired, creating their own personalized learning schedules, was simple. "We know we can design on paper a house for people, but will it be permanent? Besides, this is fun!" Yes, straight A engineering students in "nonacademic" shop class—enjoying learning. How has the Gates Foundation promoted fun, and of what value are their politician-friend requirements? The classroom math and science curriculum sequences by the Traditionalists make no sense.

The Gates Foundation has supported traditional schools with money to foster higher test scores in science, math, and reading—not "nonacademic" curriculum. Politicians and school people profess they will look good if the United States can just rise to 1-2-3 rather than 19-20-21 world standings in comparative international tests. Their focus has never been on humaneness, providing options, looking for innovative ways to help learners. The Traditionalists never seriously looked for the causes of student discontent and lack of interest in doing well on standardized tests.

To gain votes, these politicians—whether Republican or Democrat—had to make schooling look better; they never considered offering options of a variety of learning systems that might be the best investment for public money. The efforts to have significantly better learning systems—rather than continue the reinforcement of traditional mandates—have ancient histories. In spite of being well into the 21st century, politicians have continued the one-size-fits-all approaches to schooling—not even education!

EDUCATOR SEARCH

The heart of the current educational dilemma is easy to identify. Where are the Visionary Army educators hiding? In England, they are very visible. Unfortunately they have not yet been able to overcome that regressive Tory Education Act. The visionaries there continue to support those community ventures attempting to influence change. The leaders of the center for Personalised Education Now (PEN) have brilliant writers and leaders taking action steps: Roland Meighan, Christopher Shute, Clive Harber, Peter Humphrey, Christopher Ball—the famous cast of thousands—but sadly they are outnumbered by the political millions.

The over one hundred books published by PEN through their Educational Heretics Press are vivid testimony. Fittingly, Robin Hood would have fit beautifully with this group headquartered in Nottingham, U.K. Perhaps he would have been able in this 21st century to lead the overthrow of the tyranny of schooling in the United Kingdom. He could have led the modern Heretics in the use of the imagination sword rather than of the ineffective efforts of the pen and tongue against a one-sided Parliament. Even Tony Blair, when prime minister, was not able to overcome the many negative politicians who refused to rescind the Tory law!

During the most recent promising years of 20th-century education in the United States, there were hundreds not only trying to change schooling, but who were actually implementing successful personalized models. They did enjoy then the support of many politicians. Education leaders were many: John Holt, Lloyd Trump, Dwight Allen, Eugene Howard, Wayne Jennings, Jonathan Kozol, Herbert Kohl, Ronald Barnes, and the multiple other Visionaries who were creating change.

They were joined by a horde of societal critics: Paul Goodman, George Leonard, Paulo Friere, Ivan Illich, Everett Reimer, Neil Postman. Literally hundreds of educators and social critics bemoaned the negatives of Traditional public education when applied to all learners.

What did happen to the 21st-century versions of 20th-century writers and doers? They continue to be verbally very visible. Confirmation can easily be located by turning on the computer for education critic websites. Ron Miller, John Gatto, Alfie Kahn, Lynn Stoddard, William Spady, and Wayne Jennings are among the choir of social-networking malcontents. Active "doers"—members of AERO (Alternative Education Resource Organization) headed by Jerry Mintz—represent those directing terrific non-schooling alternatives programs. Descriptions of their implementation successes could fill a big book.

Humane politicians, though outnumbered, are willing to join as leaders with humane educators. However, to remain in office, they need assurance that learning Visionaries are seriously committed to the overthrow of the disastrous schooling solutions imposed by the tyrants. Thus the resistance armies advocating learning have a priority task: strongly unite educational heretics not only in the fifty states but worldwide, to support political and social critics.

It is essential in the second decade of the 21st century once again to don that famous white suit and use weapons, not words. What has happened to the efforts to unify ACTION against the continuing election of the misinformed politicians of the 21st century? What has led to the hiring of misguided school people with no vision, only blind commitment to convention?

CRITIC SEARCH

For evidence, crank up the websites, visit archives, and browse through used bookstores. The sources of societal critics against the traditionally accepted system of schooling are overwhelming. They have written beautiful, thoughtful, true insights regarding the harsh realities, but like the Visionary learning advocates, have not joined a "march" on Congress. To their credit, they have recorded the cry for personalized learning systems. Unfortunately, conventional schooling has been allowed to become worse for the majority.

The comments of the many societal critics of yesterday, the previously quoted Albert Einstein, Bertrand Russell, Winston Churchill, John Stuart Mill, Oscar Wilde, Nelson Mandela, Rita Sherman, Margaret Mead, Alfred Whitehead, Buckminster Fuller, Paul Goodman, Ivan Illich, "Charlie Brown," and a continuing litany of others, document reality. Ironically, the recent website articles against schooling traditions have only repeated the ideas for successful change prescribed by these "ancients" four decades before the end of the 20th century.

The views of the vast army of the new second decade societal critics are well summarized in a piece by insightful *Washington Post* writer Marion Brady. In his 2011 essay "An Any-Century Curriculum," he combined valid comments (paraphrased here): Our schools are stuck on a performance plateau. Even the best fail to hook the natural curiosity of students. Take away report cards, certificates, diplomas, attendance laws, parental pressures, and community expectations, and the schools of America would fall apart. Something is seriously wrong when the desired drive to learn is intrinsic, but the attempts to educate the young rely so heavily on fear and other extrinsic motivators. Doing with greater determination what is already wrong is not going to make it right. Raising standards, playing with class schedules, eliminating social promotion, administering more standardized tests, cutting class size, extending the school year, concentrating on the basics, facilitating school closures, establishing more alternative schools, installing exotic technology, or firing any of the other currently popular but traditional "silver bullets" provide no answers. These steps might bring marginal temporary improvements, but will make no significant lasting gains in the quality of the intellect!

Brady states that the answer to improvement is changing the curriculum. The Visionary Army members would wholeheartedly agree that all his criticisms of the present division of curriculum into parts are correct. However, most would not agree with his proposals of how to fix the dilemma. He devises complicated diagrams and grids to illustrate his concept of systemic relationships.

The majority of futurists would state that the designs look too much like Traditionalist "charts"! They believe that the answer to *Declaring War Against Schooling* curriculum is as simple as developing personalized learning for everyone. They opine that Brady, like other critics, often develops more complicated designs that are not understood or on target; they do agree, though, with his overall criticisms of schooling.

Visionaries also join the Brady observation that those who are playing the central role in education reform do not understand "educating." He criticizes the influence of the business roundtable, Chamber of Commerce, corporate interests, and the financing of Traditionalist politicians—cheered on by clueless mainstream media outlets. Visionary learning specialists have not been given a seat at the table of Traditionalist decisions. The big names in developing second-decade educational policy—Arne Duncan, Bill Gates, Joel Kline, Eli Broad, and, yes, Barack Obama—were not even educators, whether with conventional or innovative views.

Visionaries agree with another Brady view. Paraphrased, he stated that there is big money to be made in standardizing the curriculum, textbooks, tests, test-prep publications, and other similar benefits to corporate America. Standardized youth grow up to be standardized workers, voters, and consumers. It is much easier to write advertising copy, political platforms, stump speeches, and execute authority and control when 'human' variability is minimized.

How do educational Visionaries use Brady—and the hundreds of other societal critic comments over many decades—to overthrow the "reign of terror" imposed by conventional robots on second-decade 21st-century learners? The recent politicians have formulated their demands over four decades of domination. It is clear. Nelson Mandela was correct: Schooling does not reflect democracy.

SEARCHES COMBINED

The controlling Traditionalists have ignored the pleas of the Visionary politicians, learning experts, and societal critics. Unfortunately, the opponents of mandating Traditional education for ALL have operated independently as individuals or small groups; they have not combined as one huge political, educational and societal voice at the national, state, or local levels.

Timid change-oriented supporters have relied on (1) technological developments and (2) brain-mind research as keys that will unlock the doors to learning. They have been so starstruck by such advances as the Tûranor PlanetSolar—the first sun-powered ship to circle the world—that they believe school people will eventually be forced to design new systems for learning. They fail to remember that in spite of mind-boggling technological advances, population growth, and cutting-edge research, most seventh graders are still locked into Traditionalist jail cells in decade two of the 21st century.

The 2011 *National Geographic* magazine population series on the "Seven Billion" is staggering. It is difficult to comprehend that to count to seven billion—one second per person—would take more than two centuries, and yet in that year seven billion text messages were sent every thirty hours in the United States alone. With the mushrooming communications advances, what does the future portend?

Another 2011 *National Geographic* series on the geologic epoch, labeled the "Anthropocene Age of Man," is also hard to believe. The facts support the problems. In 1800, Mexico City had the fifth largest world metropolitan population but covered only a fraction of the surrounding geography. By 2011, the density figure was 50 percent higher using the same land—and still rising. The growth globally in the crowded shantytowns in urban centers creates an urgent need for clean water and sanitation. What do such dramatic statistics mean for the field of schooling? What is the future of education for shantytown children?

In a field related to education, brain-mind research is continuing to expand; some is difficult-to-understand theory, but researchers are trying. Dr. Liana Mattulich of Argentina has advanced theories on psycho-physiological technologies and processes that she tentatively labeled the Exceptional Performance Training System. Credit must be acknowledged for these efforts; there is no doubt much more will be known regarding the process of learning in the near-term future—but what is the effect of schooling on children of 2010–2020?

VOLCANIC ERUPTIONS

How do these jumbled combinations of political, schooling, societal, and scientific factors merge? It is simple to begin: locate learning-oriented 21st-century politicians. The reverse side of the coin is the difficulty of changing hundred-year-old traditionally controlled systems.

Political dilemmas continue in every field, not just education. Why do young men in the military serve for twenty years protecting the shores of America, but retain only 50 percent of their pay upon retirement. At the same time, while politicians usually stay in relatively safe environments with excellent health care, they receive retirement based upon full pay, even if they serve only one term in Congress. These politicos have specifically exempted themselves from many of the laws passed onto others—such as exemption from prosecution for sexual harassment or reductions resulting from reduced health care reforms for the working person. Most drive expensive tax-funded cars while in office.

This 21st-century mentality of politicians recalls the 1633 conflict in England between Caucasian Anglicans and Caucasian Puritans. In the same period in colonial America, the early brutal treatment of Native Americans—especially by the Puritans—triggered two hundred years of terrible Indian wars. Do such politics make sense? Does the American Civil War reflect politicians again? Battles during the colonial period in the new United States involved horrible scores of deaths among the French, Spanish, English, Dutch, and Indian peoples—all based on efforts for political domination.

A few events could be justified; upon reflection, most were wrong. These battles were not led by Middle Eastern terrorists or African despots. The early military years of the beloved George Washington were not marked by stories of the "cherry tree" lad but, instead, by brutality and poor judgment.

Currently in the Middle East, Pakistan is a stark modern reminder of what potentially lies ahead. As environmentalist Lester Brown reminds, in 2011 the temperature reached a record 128 degrees Fahrenheit in the southern area of the country. The Pakistan population of 185 million is squeezed into a space only 8 percent of the area of the United States. Ninety percent of the forests are gone. The livestock population of 149 million well exceeds the 103 million in America. Yet their military budget is fifteen times more than for education and forty-four times the budget for health services.

What have the local and global politicians done to address these conditions, not only in Pakistan, but worldwide? Is there really any hope?

What can the common person expect from the "poor" rich politicians and the billionaire corporation executives? Not much, as proven by the investigations of the 2008–2011 American financial crises. Senators Carl Levin (D-MI) and Tom Coburn (R-OK) presented the 2011 report from the Senate Committee for Investigations. It proved the reckless, risk-taking, and rampant conflict of interests on the part of big banks and regulatory leaders—yet those involved had scored well on schooling tests. These executives are just people who have been allowed to benefit themselves; they and their political friends closed their eyes to the fraudulent credit-rating agencies too.

On the positive caring side, these individuals are being reported by colleagues. But where was the congressional oversight that could have prevented thousands losing their homes? Is there—again—any hope for help from lawmakers?

CURRENT POLITICIANS

Forward to 21st-century education politicians. The wars over ongoing policies, though nonviolent to date, demonstrate constant conflict beyond four hundred years of settling the fifty states. Historically, most global political wars and corporate corruptions were unnecessary and unfair.

Will corporations ever be honest in their advertising? In education, were segregated schools, buses, and restaurants defensible as late as the 1950s and 1960s in the United States? Can such education conflicts be resolved with humaneness? Will education disputes ever be settled with humaneness? Will ongoing bitterness in society ever be resolved? If Visionaries are to repeal required negative schooling and move toward positive optional learning, individuals must merge their concerns. Can communities create group solutions that enable deviations from the mandated hard-to-comprehend laws passed in the name of improved education?

Successful change should be achieved without more "wars." Visionaries can establish new realities without battles if both political and school leaders can comprehend the stupidity of such political battles as between the Puritans and Anglicans four hundred years ago. Visionaries should find reasonable members of the Senate and House of Representatives. Difficult? Not with all the available social networking. They can do the same with their home-state legislature members. Find those who will listen to explanations and implementation plans. Convince them that, as politicians, there is urgency to stand against negative schooling, and help lead toward positive learning.

The 1960s/1970s in Colorado, Minnesota, South Dakota, Missouri, California, Arizona, Florida, Michigan, and Massachusetts—among others—proved that politicians can learn, can listen, and can prove to be truly humane for all their constituents related to education. Current sympathetic politicians and numerous school people trapped in the confines of real politics can give permission and support for creating nontraditional practices in education.

A review of the past four decades documents that positive politicians and educational Visionaries were caught by surprise attacks. They failed to resist with "boxing gloves" if necessary. Traditionalist politicians and school people maintained control. They not only eliminated the gains and potentials—the existing advances made during the Golden Years—but imposed even stricter negative mandates. They have been as bad (except without rifles) as the Germans who imposed one-size war practices on the Polish people. In 2020, cannot humane education visions prevail?

COMMON GROUND

There is the reality of not only hope but true ACTION possibilities. There are politicians who are fair, honest, and humane; they can be located, as were those who supported change in educational yesteryears. Visionary Army members have that priority: find these individuals, provide them with information for success, present valid evaluation tools (other than standardized tests), and ensure them support when they battle the reactionary Traditionalists. They can open doors for 20th-century schooling to become 21st-century learning. These positive politicians can insist on a reversal of current policies. Success is achievable—but ACTION is required NOW—not in another hundred years. Both Traditional and Visionary options can be supported.

Traditional Army leaders believe they are seeking to improve what they call education. Visionary Army leaders say no—their mandates are just schooling, not education. In the debate can be the vision of Helen Parkhurst: "Let us think of a school as a laboratory where pupils themselves are the experimenters, not the victims of an intricate and crystallized system. Let us think of a school as a place where communities prevail . . . as a real experience. . . . It is then no longer school—it is life."

The purpose of this book is to force a merger between schooling and learning advocates to create new education systems for tomorrow, beginning today! It is time for both Traditional and Visionary politicians to reach a common ground to free students, teachers, parents, critics, researchers—everyone interested in what has been labeled education—to devise options, not mandates, that can provide learning excitement for the future of humankind.

> I have not done a full survey or review of education systems around the world so that the views I express are based upon personal experience. I would say that all education systems I've had contact with are a disgrace and a disaster.

—Edward de Bono

Chapter Twelve

Successful Action

Schoolmaster to Peter: "Don't you want to come to school, young man?"
Peter to Schoolmaster: "No sir, thank you . . . you see, I'm so busy."
—Rita Sherman

SCHOOLING CONTROL

Declaring War Against Schooling focuses on centuries-old American dreams: democracy, freedom of choice, humane caring for persons and animals. Central to achieving these goals is the field labeled EDUCATION. The constant referrals to the conflicts between those considered educational Visionaries and those described as Traditionalists have been necessary. The beautiful, simple-to-understand descriptions of what American Education should be have not been achieved. In fact, the efforts to reach the goals have fallen further behind than ever from the dream!

Congress, state legislatures, local school boards in recent years have never comprehended the concepts of personalizing learning or personalized learning paths. Most of these politician officials have been joined by submissive school people who have let politics control what students should learn, how and when they should know the content, and how many tests they should take to demonstrate proficiency.

If the scores do not measure Traditionalist expectations, fire the teachers and/or close the schools. There has been little effort to create alternative avenues toward the future. The focus has been only on the results of numbers compiled by a computer to illustrate comparison group rankings for a schooling system. The tests have nothing to do with individual learners and their growth as persons.

Now is the time for a redesign of schooling—or more importantly, for a transformation toward new learning paths. Unlike the fleeting Camelot of the past, the moment can transition to an ever-evolving permanent future that does not relapse: "Don't let it be forgot, that once there was a spot, for one brief, shining moment that was known as Camelot."

Most ironic, to achieve the change, after a hundred years of conflict, those who consider themselves educational Visionaries or those who have been labeled Traditionalists must join forces to overcome the political control of schooling and return it to the hands of learning leaders. The unifying agreements are the focus on individual children—not test scores—and freedom of choice for all learners.

Throughout *Declaring War Against Schooling*, evidence is given that the long-existing conventional wisdoms have allowed very few individuals to reach their full potential. Schooling certainly does not fit the disillusioned "below average" youth; it seldom excites the "average" attendees, and reflects only boredom for the majority of the "above average" college-bound learners. In short, schooling is not working effectively for almost 100 percent. The overwhelming numbers—whether A- or D-evaluated students— could shine with much more luster if learning programs were personalized.

Politicians are faced with the necessity of confronting the realities of 2020. No longer is the system of schooling appropriate for 21st-century learners—of all ages. New paths for learning and the freedom to choose the most beneficial for each and every one are on the horizon. Politicians can be taught universal lessons related to education, whether global or local examples; they should apply them to the future of learning in America.

Understanding politician mentality is essential. If educators of all visions unify, in spite of their many diverse opinions, they can defeat politically imposed rituals. The barriers toward overcoming "what exists" are formidable, but success is achievable. The mindsets of most politicians, who are intent on remaining in office or advancing to another, cause many to realize they often must rely on support from educators. Globally and nationally, there are universal conditions that do affect locally made decisions pertaining to the "little red schoolhouse."

UNIVERSAL OVERSIGHT

"If you can dream it, you can do it" is a statement most often attributed to Walt Disney. It is a noble aspiration, and so often a reality—a philosophy to be pursued. Numbers of inventors have followed this path in developing electric light systems, telephones and iPods, steam engines, submarines, space stations, computers, personalized (yes) learning systems—and in the world of entertainment, Disneyland locations.

In the world of global politics, however, the "if you can dream" concept has not proved to be true. The ugly head of selfishness has prevented the elimination of societal poverty and peasant illiteracy. Can the "if you can dream it, you can do it" attitude ever be applied universally to education? The response appears to be "yes," but not in this lifetime, if greedy national and global politicians remain in control of armies, finances, and, yes, learning systems.

The country of Haiti serves as a good example of the ineffectiveness and wrong decisions made by politicians, not only in the United States but worldwide regarding old-fashioned politics, starvation, illiteracy, and other combinations—but especially the relationships of these conditions to education.

HAITIAN ODYSSEY

The 2010 devastating earthquake in Haiti was not the first, but perhaps the worst, of the many Haitian disasters of earthquakes, hurricanes, and politics. Before this last event, Haitians—citizens of the first independent Caribbean country—demonstrated the political insanities, the futilities of American aid, and the ineffectiveness of United Nations resolutions.

A 1988 speech by Marie Bogat, an American director of the Port-au-Prince K–12 Union School, summarized thirty years of her Haitian experiences of hurricanes, revolutions, palace coups, school closings, evacuations, naval bombardments, political upheavals, and moving the school under duress for political reasons. She closed her one hour of factual stories with a quote of hope from Ulysses: "Come, my friends, 'tis not too late to seek a newer world."

A young teacher from New York, Marie Bogat went to Haiti for a short overseas experience. What she witnessed became a lifetime personal and professional goal of trying to help students and their families through the good and the bad years. After retiring from Port-au-Prince to Florida, Dr. Bogat "unretired" to create exciting approaches for teacher education at the Union Institute and University. The results of these better programs for future teachers brought her many distinguished honors. She, as one of the Visionaries, tried to think globally—Haiti conditions—and act locally—Union School—to overcome tradition.

Despite her efforts in Florida, the state still has the conventional seventh-grade syndrome. Ironically, the original 5–8 middle school design was spawned by Dr. William Alexander, professor at the University of Florida, but no true middle schools now exist in the Sunshine State. Will politicians ever allow Visionary structures to be permanently implemented to improve learning opportunities for students?

Unbelievably, with all the recent sadness of the earthquakes and displaced persons, the 2011 Haitian presidential election was again marked by fraud! Illustrating these ongoing occurrences, a half-century earlier in 1963, "Papa Doc" Duvalier stayed in power through orders for his armed "henchmen" to round up truckloads of defenseless peasants and force them to Port-au-Prince—accompanied by demands to cheer every word by candidate Duvalier and vote for his reelection in this "democratic nation."

Sitting next to Papa Doc was a leading opposition candidate, Alain Laraque—with a gun at his back—waiting his turn to announce his resignation as a candidate and enthusiastically endorse Duvalier. If he had wavered, he and his family would have been found in the cemetery. The U.S. government (yes, politicians again) knew of the situation but decided such a tragic country as Haiti was not worth the risk of further intervention.

Later in 1963, when Duvalier imposed martial law and curfews, after the kidnap attempt on his thirteen-year-old son, hundreds of innocent civilians were killed during the search for the organizers. Washington sent the USS *Boxer* into the harbor, loaded with marines, but they could not land, for Duvalier stated he would slaughter the large number of Americans living in Haiti.

Three centuries pass (19th, 20th, 21st); Disney was once again proved wrong. Politicians cannot dream that change can be humanely accomplished. The bloody overthrow of the French in 1804 gained "independence" but also created nothing but problems. In 1916, the United States had to send the Marines to quell the looming disorder. Now it is 2020. What relationship do two hundred years of Haitian histories and earthquakes have to do with education politics in the United States? The response is again simple: politicians!

POLITICS CONTINUED

A 2011 report in California—one of the more earthquake-prone of the fifty states—proved that state regulators have routinely failed to enforce the landmark Field Act to ensure that children and teachers would not occupy buildings with structural flaws. The Field regulations were enacted after the disastrous Long Beach earthquake of 1933, which destroyed or severely damaged 230 school buildings near the epicenter. Thousands of children would have been killed if the quake had occurred during school hours.

The chief regulator of construction standards for public schools ignored 1,100 building flaws red-flagged by supervisors from the Division of State Architecture during the ten-year period of 2000 to 2010. The problems were logged, but nothing was done, though the regulators have the "police power of the state" to enforce Field Act compliance. Where was the political oversight? The answer: a cozy relationship between politicians and the school building industry!

Enforcement was plagued with bureaucratic chaos and citations lost in a swamp of paperwork. The Department of General Services described this "mess" as simply ten years of bookkeeping issues, yet tens of thousands of children and teachers attend schools specified as unsafe by the Field Act regulations.

Traditionalist politicians and school administrators have often been proved not to be trustworthy in enforcing learning improvements. As the Visionaries point out, more math and reading tests—which amount to little—are not going to improve life. Haiti and California are only two examples of inept systems of global schooling. Local school board members run for office for power, their own point of view, or as a stepping stone to higher office—not really to help most learners.

It is well known how unethical most corporations are, as shown by their perhaps not illegal—but immoral—transactions such as selling a consumer a tire with a guarantee without explaining the many caveats, exemplified by the need to return a damaged tire ONLY to the seller. Does much need to be written regarding the entirety of the conditions in the Middle East?

Regardless of the final results of the 2011 outbursts, what is the 2020 outlook for the school children in Libya, Egypt, Tunisia, Syria, Iran, Iraq, Afghanistan, Yemen, Bahrain, Jordan, Lebanon, Sudan, and the Ivory Coast? Why, since 1947, have international and local POLITICIANS—despite repeated and sometimes sincere efforts—not been able to solve the Palestine-Israel dilemma, or even Kashmir or Tibet? Again, Disney appears to be wrong. If you dream it, you cannot always do it!

The uprisings in the many 2011 Middle East conflicts were said to have been enhanced by such gimmicks as Twitter, Facebook, iPods. No doubt these helped rally thousands through instant communication. Forgotten sometimes is that the 1989 parade of protesting Germans did not have these instruments. They were certainly not available for the thousands marching for civil rights in the 1960s. How did these marchers receive the word to assemble? How did Paul Revere communicate?

Was the ridiculous 2011 budget stalemate in the United States Congress aided by the use of Twitter? How much help has instant communication provided for children in South Africa born with HIV, or for the slave workers imported from Bangladesh to work the Libyan oil fields, often unpaid, or the future of the desolate hundred-by-fifty-mile "empty quarter" near Chernobyl? What aid to improve such conditions has been provided by politicians? Homelessness and unsatisfactory foster care for children continue, while many adults double-dip from federal retirement funds.

Are these many global issues truly related to education and school-aged youth—especially in America? The response, of course, is yes! A reflective 2011 cartoon portrayed an elementary student with his D report card, contrasted with a heavily armed Libyan rebel. The caption read: "Which underperforming person receives more additional United States aid?" How can schooling expect to be improved when it is part of a scheme of illogical global, state, and local conditions designed by politicians, not by educators?

REFLECTING RESPONSES

Do traditional lawmakers and school people provide controlled, dignified, reasonable responses to the many societal and educational issues? Do they offer to listen to the opposition? NO! Again, the irony is that the educational Visionaries cannot overcome the majority of "bad" politicians without the support of educational Traditionalists. The 2011 cartoon by Stahler of the *Columbus Dispatch* verifies the hot air of politicians. In it, President Richard Nixon and every one since—Ford, Carter, Reagan, Bush, Clinton, Bush, and Obama—are repeating exactly the same line: "We must reduce our dependency on Mideast oil." The opposite has been true. The nation has increased its dependency. How can educators overcome political-education slogans with no evidence of ACTION?

Local and national politicians have become increasingly stringent with their mandates. Most charter schools are hanging on by a thread. They are a nuisance: their test scores are too low or too high, but either way they divert funds and facilities from the local district. They are not allowed major deviations from the conventional formats. Waldorf charters are attacked by religious zealots who claim publicly funded charter schools are being used to promote spiritualism and mysticism. Early-reading test scores are lower, for the Waldorf system does not force reading in kindergarten. Modest Montessori approaches are frowned upon, for public money is funding a private school philosophy.

Reflecting on the first Montessori School, which was in Amsterdam, the well-educated German soldiers—ordered by their political leaders—invaded the site and eventually killed 173 of the 193 enrolled children. The stories of the twenty who managed to survive have been recorded by a current Amsterdam Montessori teacher, and translated and enhanced by one of the survivors—Hannie Voyles. Anne Frank attended this school! Again, again, again—will Race to the Top and higher math and science programs translate to improving the world human condition?

Education unions will not help, for many of the charter teachers do not join the district organization. School board members who, before charter approval, force restrictions preventing Visionary deviations are merely politicians too. Again, the continuing dilemma: how do educators merge to force optional learning systems? How do they say to politicians—national, state, or local—NO to their misguided edicts?

Secretary of Education Duncan, a political Traditionalist in the purest sense, advocated replacing the separate state tests with one fifty-state national assessment—forcing more billions to be spent on a paper product—and making the corporate testing industry rich beyond belief. Obama is going to "fix" the schooling system! Will his "agenda" authorities ever listen to opposing views?

UNETHICAL BEHAVIOR

When the March 28, 2011, edition of *USA Today* can headline a three-page report without doubt on unethical District of Columbia (D.C.) administration testing procedures, Shakespeare was right:

"Something is rotten in the state of Denmark." In the analyses by several testing experts of data secured through the Freedom of Information Act, extraordinarily high numbers of erasures on D.C. standardized tests were discovered. In fact, 103 public schools—more than half of the district total—had erasure rates that raised previous test score averages that could not have been obtained by traditional methods of schooling in one or two years.

Forty-one of the D.C. schools were flagged in 2010 by CTB/McGraw-Hill which supplied and administered the tests. Their analysis concluded that there were significantly high numbers of wrong answers changed to the correct ones on math and reading tests. McGraw-Hill only looked for "beyond doubt" erasure schools, overlooking many in the district. The head of the Washington D.C. Teachers' Union compared it to a Ponzi scam: "If your test scores improve, you make more money; if they don't, you get fired."

The District of Columbia is not the only city with possible malfeasance regarding standardized test scores. In Georgia, high erasures from wrong to right answers triggered a criminal investigation. The Georgia Bureau of Investigation interrogated staff at fifty-eight Atlanta schools where there were statistically significant rates of such erasures. The Traditionalist politicians forced cheating—wherever it may have occurred in all fifty state jurisdictions—by passing beyond-insane testing pressures linked to distribution of federal and state money to "high achieving" schools and by firing teachers where possible if their classroom test scores were low.

Worse is the fact that Traditionalist school people caved in to the pressures from the politicians. They should have refused and just said NO to the legislatures. Committed educators knew that the mandated laws of the past twenty years have been wrong; they failed to "stand tall." Many reverted to potentially undesirable procedures to maintain a false positive image for parents, themselves, and the community being served.

The Visionary Army members were wrong, too. They failed to alert all citizens of the damage to children and learning inflicted by these tests. They wrote, they spoke, but once more repeated, they did not ACT; they did not go on strike. Individually many directed their own small school or were content to write more publications. Visionaries were as guilty as the Traditionalist school people!

Further, numerous college professors offered to raise student grades regardless of test scores—if, for example, they helped raise money for the College Foundation Fund. High school teachers provided incentives and prizes to their students—and a raise in their final grade if they did well on the mandated tests; the offers involved improving their class ranking for graduation and college entrance. The *Bee* newspaper, in April, 2011, which documented these procedures in the Sacramento, California, vicinity revealed such practices in many of the fifty states. The headline read: "Did Schools Flunk Ethics: Higher Grades Are Dangled Before Students?"

Obviously such practices in the name of education cannot remain part of the American dream. To change to a higher level of humaneness, both the Visionary and Traditional armies of EDUCATORS must merge and not allow unethical schooling practices to continue. By discovering common grounds as learning leaders, they can present a united front to politicians, boards, parents, and students.

Communities must be told that many of the old practices of schooling (measuring success by comparative testing) cannot continue. "We are the educators—you are the politicians. We will work to create a humane system called learning." This can become a unification slogan. But how? That question becomes the final challenge in ending the 100 Years War Against Learning. This time, the combined campaigns search must lead to SUCCESSFUL ACTION.

MANY SIZES

To achieve success, the one-size-fits-all schooling mentality of the past three decades would change to a belief that many sizes should fit all! How do both Traditionalists and Visionaries combine to present a unified front—as friends, not enemies—to tell the politicians that the hundred years of conflict are finally resolved. There is no longer a War Against Learning.

As with the end of World War II, Germany and Japan are not the enemy. Instead, as Allies, there is a common commitment with visions of continuing to search for better approaches for the 21st century and beyond. Gone is the issue of "reforming schooling." The agreement focus is personalizing learning. This combined step creates successful ACTION—the end result of *Declaring War Against Schooling.*

There remain those much-discussed global priorities. Regardless of political views and past and present schooling or learning differences, education remains as a major global dilemma. The reality reminder is that most people cannot live much beyond five minutes without air, five days without water, or five weeks without food. The fact that former U.S. Olympic track star Louie Zamperini and two companions made it through a grueling forty-seven days in a small raft after crashing in the Pacific during World War II was a miracle to be sure; they did have the occasional intermittent rain showers, a small shark, and later raw albatross—meat and feathers.

This ordeal is difficult to comprehend. When captured, Zamparini was brutally beaten almost daily in Japanese prison camps; his survival was even more astounding. As with Japan and America, there are those essential reconciliations and partnerships between the former enemies to overcome the long-standing feud following Pearl Harbor. Michael Burleigh wrote: "Those who did evil believed they were doing good." Continuing totalitarian schooling only reinforces fixed rules.

More than ever, the two educational enemies—the Visionaries and the Traditionalists—as educators, not as school people, must jointly oppose political control of schooling systems. The future for learners of all ages is precious. In the early 21st century—already into its second decade—educators and politicians must resolve differences which otherwise could lead to a civil war over learning.

ACTION STEPS

1. Those who commit to changing schooling to learning join to create a plan to—ironically—overthrow Traditionalist American politicians. Educators, not politicos, must assume leadership for designing and implementing the best approaches for helping people of all walks of life who want to follow their own humane passionate paths toward positive individual, group, and societal living.

2. In planning, there are no more speeches or debates over implementation methods for personalized learning. That issue is quickly resolved. The focus is an agreement for ACTION to demand that politicians step aside. Learning advocates—not lawmakers—are the leaders to create responses to "what next"!

3. If the politicians will not gracefully step aside, a coordinated four-week national strike is formed against the political establishment trying to retain control over schooling decisions. Coverage is provided by the major media outlets. The public can then comprehend and support the battle for the future of learning, not schooling!

4. Participating leaders of the now unified Educators for Learning meet with politicians to confirm they will no longer adhere to past legislative edicts—except those with life- threatening safety and health issues—as with the 2011 Japanese earthquake.

5. If "force" is required, as with the 1960s Civil Rights marches, then state leadership groups as, for illustration, the Minnesota Association for Alternative Programs, MUST ACT! Their nine hundred educator members, accompanied by parents, students, and community members, accept the risk involved, and ascend the steps of the St. Paul capitol building and remind all that they are determined to regain the status Minnesota once held as the number one state advocating for learning, not schooling.

6. National educational leaders meet with identified humane politicians who agree with the philosophy of personalizing learning programs. Together—whether Republican or Democrat, or other potential Visionary offshoots—they promote goals similar to those proposed "long ago" by President Johnson. Extensive portfolios of a hundred research and experimentation studies are presented, documenting the fallacies of one-size-fits-all schooling and testing mandates!

7. Learning advocates "tell the world" that political schooling decisions are no longer accepted. There is a "Just Say No" zero tolerance policy that indicates they will not follow traditional, ill-fated efforts of the political world to impose bad legislation denying personalized learning.

8. The new unified educators insist on the immediate cessation of nonsensical prior political decisions that prevent learning programs of choice. One "now" step is to refuse to abide by the massive illogical testing mandates. This alone will relieve the pressure for cheating, create honest discussions, and save billions of dollars to use for learning research—not to line the pockets of corporate testing companies.

9. Educators—not politicians—look for immediate, easy, cost-effective changes to begin the Action process. As often verified, changing from a graded to a nongraded system of organizing for learning costs nothing. "Pied Piper" educators easi-

ly adapt and are enthusiastic. They explain the benefits of the changes to parents and communities. Leave extreme traditional parents and teachers with an option that they can continue as a choice, not a mandate, with business as usual.

10. Eventual NASA Space Center educational research projects are funded to continue the efforts to know all that can be known regarding the best learning avenues for each individual. Open minds are kept for safe but sometimes very experimental procedures for volunteers—as with the astronaut philosophy. A start can be made with such inexpensive investigations as to whether iPads should join with—or replace—crayons. Do iPads make a difference? Most of the big projects would be major designs of potential better learning options.

11. With explanations, communities can realize that, as with multiple places of worship for the many interpretations of religion, by accepting diverse learning choices 24/7/365—including those by "agnostics"— America is finally reaching the educational dream of the "founding fathers." Their sometimes diverse views of societal freedoms were perhaps the major cause of the break with England. The settlers tried to establish new hope for better living, learning, and pioneering futures for people.

12. *Declaring War Against Schooling* draws realities from the 1500s to the 2000s. The experiences of these six hundred years must be communicated to the various publics for an understanding of why the past must lead to the future. These six centuries have provided time for the 21st-century Visionaries to ensure freedom of learning in the field considered EDUCATION.

"What is the use of a book," thought Alice, "without pictures or conversations?"
—Lewis Carroll

Revolution will occur in education too. We will move away from a system that assumes every child of a particular age moves at the same pace in every subject, and instead develop a system directed to the particular talents, interests, and time needs of every student.

—Anthony Blair

Epilogue

Personal Commitment

American education is one of the most wasteful things in the whole organization of life. Ask most well-informed parents about the progress of their child in school and you receive a cry of discontent and helpless protest. The letters of evidence I have come from college professors to street laborers. . . . . The education on which we spend so much money and boast so loudly in our communities is so indifferent to the individual—and thus a fearfully wasteful and costly process. We could possibly endure if it did no good. But it does not stop there—it is demoralizing the mental habits of the nation. . . . The teachers are doing their best, but the results are discouraging.
—Adolf A. Berle

MOVING FORWARD

The brilliant Adolf Berle was unfortunately correct in his assessment of schooling. However, his negative views can lead to the search for a positive future for learning. New horizons in education are obtainable if leadership is found to eliminate the current TYRANNY of oppressive schooling mandates.

There is no need for such shameful books as *Letter to a Teacher*, where the peasant schoolboys of Barbiana, Italy, wrote that schooling is a war against the poor. This reflection can be expanded to affirm that traditional schooling is a war against most learners of all ages and backgrounds.

The urgency of changing educational systems is global. The fate of the world and its inhabitants in the year 2100 will eventually be determined by students. In the spring 2011 Blue Planet United *Population Press*, an article, "Planet and Population" by Sir David Attenborough, presented a more than abundantly clear portrait.

In 1960 there were "only" three billion people on earth. In 2010 there were seven billion; this number was growing by 80 million a year. In exploding Pakistan, the 1950 count was 39 million; by 2050, the population projection was for 330 million. Egypt in 2010 counted 80 million; by 2050 the count is expected to reach 177 million. Iran contributes 34 percent of the world growth, while the United States figure is 21 percent. Partial causes of the Middle East uprisings were overpopulation, environmental destruction, and rising food prices; each threatens nation failure. A few countries are awakening; Australia now has a cabinet position—the Sustainable Population Minister—to address the problem.

David Attenborough continued his views. He stated: "Environmental and social problems . . . not only create the potential extinction of even more people, but also animal and plant disasters. . . . Added to the list are everyday concerns, as traffic congestion, oil prices, health services, megacities, migration, underemployment, desertification, famine, violent weather, acidification, and rainforest destruction."

In June 2011, Philippe Cousteau, CEO of EcoOceans, reminded us how near humans are to destroying life in the oceans and thus themselves, but there are solutions if people globally act before it is too late. Education obviously cannot solve all these problems, but if ever there is a chance to emerge a significantly better planet, it is now. It involves improved commitment to resolve these conditions through learning, not schooling. Yes, biologists, chemists, and oceanographers are required to lead in reducing carbons (cognitive), but those with human qualities (affective) are needed even more.

Politicians and educators of today should heed a "pass or fail" lesson from the sixteenth president of the United States, Abraham Lincoln. His astounding rise to leadership is well documented in *Team of Rivals* (Doris Goodwin). Upon being the surprise winner of the 1860 election, he surmised that the best way to achieve his goals was NOT to handpick his close supporters, but instead to recruit the talents of his best rivals to form a cabinet that could, by consensus, chart the best possible path for the future of the country.

He selected his eminent Republican Party rivals for essential posts: William Seward as secretary of state, Salmon Chase as secretary of the treasury, and Edward Bates as attorney general. These leaders were joined by distinguished Democrats: Gideon Wells as secretary of the navy, Montgomery Blair as postmaster general, and Edwin Stanton as secretary of war. The capacity of Lincoln to gather opponents to compose this most unusual cabinet allowed him to marshal their talents, win the war, and begin the reconstruction period.

Certainly forecasting the potentials of global 2050, when 2010 kindergarteners will only be forty-five, should present a compelling demand for new educational systems. The 1860 era of Lincoln—only ninety years past—and his ability to rally support even among his rivals offer profound lessons for creating new directions for education in the United States.

Such portraits should also eventually lead to a nationwide change in media coverage of educational issues. Currently most media outlets know little about learning—only schooling. An example is the May 15, 2011, CNN program "Education for America." One comment was that most youth should take calculus and physics to move the United States from twenty-seventh to first in mathematics and science. This ludicrous solution could not be further from the truth. CNN concentrates on budget and test-score issues with "important people." This network and competing outlets seldom present "the other side of the story" related to schooling versus learning.

The 2011 Mississippi River flooding again reinforces the necessity of raising the "what if" questions. "What if" a hundred-year flood does occur, as in Minot, North Dakota? What could be done to prevent many—not all—natural disasters from causing severe disruption in the lives of people?

Which individuals, as a unified army in the second decade of the 21st century, will become both the pen and sword of Joan of Arc, and the Team of Rivals of Lincoln to pursue *learning, not schooling*? Educational leaders should challenge and work in concert with supportive politicians to form a humane commitment toward significantly better opportunities for learners. Hopefully success in North America can create a global spin-off.

There should be much optimism for positive 21st-century outcomes for Personalizing Learning Futures. Who—among those with visions of significantly different and better opportunities for learners—will mobilize Visionaries and take giant steps leading to nationwide ACTION?

> What we want to see is the child in pursuit of knowledge—not knowledge in pursuit of the child.
> —George Bernard Shaw

REWARD POSTER

WANTED: Alive, Visionary Education Leaders
PURPOSE: To ensure choices of personalized learning options for ALL LEARNERS

NEEDED: A strong posse to capture the one-size-fits-all traditional school people and politicians to force them to LISTEN

REQUIRED: A committed SHERIFF and DEPUTIES to lead the posse against the powerful opponents entrenched in their hideouts.

OUTCOME: Conviction of the outlaws, forcing them to rescind their *mandated for ALL* bad testing, curriculum, and rituals, and thus creating educational alternatives for everyone.

PAYMENT: Satisfaction of providing an environment of democracy and freedom FOR ALL LEARNERS to select their personalized learning designs.

DANGERS: Failure is not possible by the POSSE, for such would allow schooling as it exists to continue, rather than encourage learning to emerge as it could and should be for the present and future.

SUPPORT: (1) State education organizations to lead a JUST SAY NO to ill-conceived policies and requirements. (2) Individuals to join actively in the overthrow of control by politicians, and return education to the hands of Learning Not Schooling leaders. (3) Parents and students who are disillusioned with schooling and willing to take a stand. (4) Teacher/administrator groups committed to providing choices for all learners.

Bibliography

REFERENCES

Ackerman, Diane. *The Zookeeper's Wife: A War Story*. W. W. Norton, New York, 2007.

Bade, William Frederic. *The Life and Letters of John Muir*. The John Muir Collections, Holt-Atherton Library, University of the Pacific, Stockton, CA, 1924.

Ballinger, Charles, and Carolyn Kneese. *School Calendar Reform: Learning in All Seasons*. Rowman & Littlefield Publishers, Lanham, MD, 2006.

Ballinger, Charles, and Carolyn Kneese. *Balancing the School Calendar*. Rowman & Littlefield Publishers, Lanham, MD, 2009.

Barnes, Ron. *Learning Systems for the Future*. Phi Delta Kappa, Bloomington, IN, 1972.

Bernstein, Emmanuel. *The Secret Revolution: A Psychologist's Adventures in Education*. Trafford Publishing, Victoria, British Columbia, Canada, 2007.

Blishen, Edward. *The School That I'd Like*. Penguin, Harmondsworth, England, 1969.

Bode, Carl. *Best of Thoreau's Journals*. Southern Illinois University Press, Carbondale, 1967.

Brown, Lester. *World on the Edge: How to Prevent Environmental and Economic Collapse*. Earth Policy Institute, Washington, DC, 2010.

Browning, Robert. "The Pied Piper of Hamelin." Browning poems, England, 1842.

Caine, Renate, and Geoffrey Caine. *Natural Learning for a Connected World*. Teachers College Press, New York, 2011.

Carswell, Evelyn, et al. *The Nongraded School*. Elementary School Principals Department, National Education Association, Washington, DC, 1968.

Cleveland, Harlan. *The Global Commons: Policy for the Planet*. University Press of America, Lanham, MD, 1990.

Combs, Arthur. *Myths in Education: Beliefs That Hinder Progress and Their Alternatives*. Allyn & Bacon, Boston, 1979.

Counts, George. *Dare the School Build a New Social Order?* John Day, New York, 1932.

Dahl, Roald. *Charlie and the Chocolate Factory*. Penguin Books, New York, 1994.

Dewey, John. *Democracy in Education*. Macmillan Publishers, New York, 1916.

Douglass, Harl. *Modern Administration of Secondary Schools,* 2nd ed. Holt, Rinehart & Winston, New York, 1991.

Duberman, Martin. *Black Mountain College: An Exploration in Community*. Dutton Publishers, New York, 1972.

Earle, Sylvia. *The World Is Blue: How Our Fate and the Ocean's Are One*. National Geographic Society, Washington, DC, 2009.

Education USA. *Individualization in Schools: The Challenge and the Options*. National School Public Relations Association, Washington, DC, 1971.

Fantini, Mario. *Public Schools of Choice*. Simon & Schuster, New York, 1974.

Forum. "Education: New Visions for the Future." Consumer Education Services, J. C. Penney Inc., New York, May 1984.

Friere, Paulo. *Pedagogy of the Oppressed*. Herder & Herder, New York, 1972.

Fuller, Buckminster. *Critical Path*. St. Martin's Press, New York, 1981.

Glines, Don. "Principals with Vision Are Needed to Make Schools Exciting Places." *NASSP Bulletin*, Reston, VA, 1992.

Goodlad, John, and Robert Anderson. *The Nongraded Elementary School*. Harcourt Brace World, New York, 1959.

Goodman, Paul. *Compulsory Mis-Education*. Vintage Books, New York, 1962.

Goodwin, Doris Kearns. *Team of Rivals: The Political Genius of Abraham Lincoln*. Simon & Schuster, New York, 2006.

Harber, Clive. *Toxic Schooling: How Schools Became Worse*. Educational Heretics Press, Nottingham, England, 2009.

Harman, Willis. *An Incomplete Guide to the Future*. The Portable Stanford Series, San Francisco Book Company, San Francisco, 1976.

Harris, Mary. *The Arts at Black Mountain*. MIT Press, Cambridge, MA, 1987.

Hemming, James. *The Betrayal of Youth*. Marion Boyars, London, 1980.

Hillenbrand, Laura. *Unbroken: A World War II Story of Survival, Resilience, and Redemption*. Random House, New York, 2010.

Holmes, Edmond. *The Tragedy of Education*. Constable & Co., London, 1913.

Holt, John. *How Children Fail*. Pitman, New York, 1964.

Holt, John. *What Do I Do on Monday?* E. R. Dutton, New York, 1970.

Huxley, Thomas H. *Science and Education*. Engel, London, 1890.

Illich, Ivan. *Deschooling Society*. Harper & Row, New York, 1971.

Jackson, Philip. *Life in the Classroom*. Holt, Rinehart & Winston, New York, 1968.

Kilpatrick, William Heard. *Remaking the Curriculum* Newson, 1936.

Leonard, George. *Education and Ecstasy*. Tarcher/Putnam, New York, 1968.

Mazer, Cary. *Bernard Shaw: A Brief Biography*. (English U Penn.) University of Pennsylvania, Philadelphia, 2010.

Meighan, Roland. *Natural Learning and the Natural Curriculum: Anybody, Any Time, Any Place, Any Pathway, Any Pace*. Educational Heretics Press, Nottingham, England, 2001.

Meighan, Roland, et al. *Damage Limitation: Trying to Reduce the Harm Schools Do to Children*. Educational Heretics Press, Nottingham, England, 2004.

Miller, Ron. *Free Schools, Free People*. State University of New York Press, Albany, 2002.

Moffett, James. *The Universal Schoolhouse*. Jossey-Bass, San Francisco, 1994.

Northwestern Bell Magazine. "MXC: A City with a Taste for Tomorrow." *Special Edition, Northwestern Bell Magazine*, Minneapolis, MN, 1972.

Nyerere, Julius. *Education for Self-Reliance*. Government Printer, Dar es Salaam, Tanzania, 1967.

Orr, David. *Ecological Literacy: Education and the Transition to a Post-Modern World*. State University of New York Press, Albany, 1992.

Postman, Neil, and Charles Weingartner. *Teaching as a Subversive Activity*. Delta, New York, 1969.

Prange, Gordon. *Miracle at Midway*. MJF Books, New York, 1982.

Reimer, Everett. *School Is Dead*. Doubleday, Garden City, NY, 1971.

Rogers, Carl. *Freedom to Learn*. Merrill, 1969.

Rogers, Everett, et al. *Change Processes in the Public Schools*. Center for the Advanced Study of Educational Aministration, University of Oregon, Eugene, 1965.

Russell, Bertrand. *On Education*. George Allen & Unwin, London, 1926.

Sarason, Seymour. *The Predictable Failure of Educational Reform*. Jossey-Bass, San Francisco, 1993.

Sarason, Seymour. *Charter Schools: Another Flawed Educational Reform*. Teachers College Press, New York, 1998.

Schorling, Raleigh, and McClusky, Howard Y. *Education and Social Trends*. Yonkers-on-Hudson, New York: World Book Company, 1936.

Schoolboys of Barbiana. *Letter to a Teacher*. Random House, New York, 1970.

Shute, Chris. *Bertrand Russell: Education as the Power of Independent Thought*. Educational Heretics Press, Nottingham, England, 2002.

Sherman, Rita. *A Mother's Letters to a Schoolmaster*. Alfred Knopf, New York, 1923.

Swift, Jonathan. *Gulliver's Travels*. Pocket Books, New York, 1996.

Theobald, Robert. *The Rapids of Change*. Knowledge Systems, Indianapolis, IN, 1987.

Trump, J. Lloyd. *A School for Everyone*. National Association of Secondary School Principals, Reston, VA, 1977.

Tyler, Ralph, and E. A. Smith. *Appraising and Recording Student Progress*. Harper, New York, 1942.

Van Til, William. *My Way of Looking at It: An Autobiography,* 2nd ed. Caddo Gap Press, San Francisco, 1996.

Vars, Gordon. *Interdisciplinary Teaching: Why and How.* National Middle Schools Association, Columbus, OH, 1993.

Voyles, Hannie (translator), and Ronald Sanders (compiler). *Storming the Tulips.* Stonebrook Publishing, St. Louis, MO, 2011

Webster, Mark, ed. *Personalized Learning: Taking Choice Seriously.* Educational Heretics Press, Nottingham, England, 2008.

Whitehead, Alfred North. *Aims of Education.* Mentor, New York, 1948.

Wirt, William. *The Great Lockout in America's Citizenship Plants.* Horace Mann School Printing Shop, Gary, IN, 1937. (Archives, Indiana University Northwest, Gary, IN)

Wolk, Ronald. *Wasting Minds: Why Our Education System Is Failing and What We Can Do About It.* Association for Supervision and Curriculum Development, Alexandria, VA, 2010.

DOCUMENTATION

In concert with the documents at the conclusion of chapter four, the following are offered as further evidence supporting the necessary transition from schooling to learning.

Arum, Richard, and Josiper Roska. *Academically Adrift: Limited Learning on College Campuses.* (Collegiate Learning Assessment, 2007). University of Chicago Press, Chicago, IL, 2010.

Barnes, Ron. *Lessons for Leaders.* The Printed Page, Phoenix, AZ, 2005.

Blue Planet United. *Population Press.* (Global Population, Poverty Statistics). P.O. Box 7918, Redlands, CA 92375. Winter 2011.

Bogat, Marie. "A Master Administrator Speaks." American Association of International Administrators, Distinguished Overseas Lecture Series, 1988.

Brady, Marion. *What's Worth Learning?* Information Age Publishers, Charlotte, NC, 2010.

Brady, Marion. *An Any-Century Curriculum.* www.marionbrady.com/documents, 2011.

Brady, Marion. "Juggernaut." *Washington Post,* Washington, DC. February 3, 2011.

Burleigh, Michael. *Moral Combat: Good and Evil in World War II.* Harper, New York, 2010.

CERC News. Research Report, "Retention of Students." California Educational Research Cooperative, School of Education, University of California-Riverside, Vol. 12, No.3. Winter 2000.

Class of 1938, Ohio State University School. *Were We Guinea Pigs?* Henry Holt, New York, 1938.

"College Bound Senior Test Scores: SAT 1999." *Fair Test Examiner*, Jamaica Plain, MA. Fall 1999.

Davis, Kenneth. *America's Hidden History*. Random House, New York, 2008.

Earth Policy Institute. (Natural Resources, Environmental Statistics). Suite 403, 1350 Connecticut Ave. NW, Washington, DC 20036.

Einstein, Albert. *The Albert Einstein Archives*. Hebrew University, Jerusalem, Israel, 2011.

Engel, Angela. *Seeds of Tomorrow*. Centennial, Colorado, www.angelaengel.com, 2011.

Evaluation of Alternative Schools. Education Research Service, Arlington, VA, 1977.

Fege, Arnold. *Public Advocacy*. "It Makes No Sense," by Yong Zhao. Public Education Network, Washington, DC. January 2011.

Finley, Warren, et al. "Ability Grouping, 1970." Center for Educational Improvement, University of Georgia, Athens. January 1971.

Friedman, Howard, et al. *The Longevity Project*. Hudson Street Press/Penguin, New York, 2011.

Gagne, Robert, et al. "Project Talent." *The School Administrator*. February 1976.

Gillum, Jack, and Marisol Bello. "When Test Scores Soured in D.C. Were the Gains Real?" *USA Today*, McLean, VA. March 28, 2011.

Jennings, Wayne. "Startling, Disturbing, Delightful Research." *Phi Delta Kappan*, Bloomington, IN. March 1977.

Johnson, Corey. "California Watch: School Protection Shaky." *Sacramento Bee*. April 8, 2001.

Lawes, Lewis. "A Challenge to the Schools." *Good Housekeeping*. September 1932.

Levin, Carl (Democratic senator from Michigan) and Tom Coburn (Republican senator from Oklahoma). "A Man-Made Economic Assault: Bipartisan Report on Causes of the Financial Crises." *U.S. Senate Investigation Report*. April 2011.

Lounsbury, John, ed. *The Junior High We Need*. Association for Supervision and Curriculum Development, Alexandria, VA, 1961.

Lounsbury, John, ed. *The Junior High We Saw*. Association for Supervision and Curriculum Development, Alexandria, VA, 1964.

National Geographic. "Population Seven Billion." *National Geographic Magazine*, Washington, DC. January 2011.

Rapp, Doris, M.D. *Is This Your Child's World?* Bantam Books, New York, 1996.

Rutter, Michael. *Fifteen Thousand Hours: Secondary Schools and Their Effect on Children*. Harvard University Press, Cambridge, MA, 1979.

Spitz, Vivien. *Doctors from Hell: The Horrific Account of Nazi Experiments on Humans*. Sentient Publications, Boulder, CO, 2005.

Spady, William. *Beyond Counterfeit Reforms*. Rowman & Littlefield, Lanham, MD, 2001.

Stanford Research Institute. *Alternative Fitness and Educational Policy*. Stanford Research Institute, Palo Alto, CA, 1970.

Toepfer, Conrad, Richard Lipka, John Lounsbury, Samuel Alessi, Craig Kridel, and Gordon Vars. *The Eight-Year Study Revisited: Lessons from the Past for the Present*. National Middle Schools Association, Columbus, OH, 1998.

UNESCO. "Declarations of the Responsibilities of the Present Generation toward Future Generations." *Future Generations Journal*, Vol. 24. New York, 1998.

Willis, Judy. "What to Do When Your Child Hates School" and Tamer Lewin, "Many States Adapt National Standards for Their Schools." *Education Revolution*, No. 62. AERO, Roslyn Heights, New York. Fall 2010.

Willis, Margaret. *Guinea Pigs Twenty Years Later*. Ohio State University Press, Columbus, OH, 1961.

Index

achievement percentages, 21
action steps now, 8, 173–175
affective domain, 17
algebra, 85
Allen, Dwight, 109
alternatives, choices of, 93
American dreams, 161
American Indian education, 95–97
Amphitheater District, Arizona, 98
Amsterdam Montessori, 169
Anderson, Robert, 136
Animal School, 2
Attenborough, David, 178
autism, 33

Ballinger, Charles, 27
Barnes, Ronald, 54
bells ringing, 22
Berle, Adolf, 177
Bernstein, Emmanuel, 130
Black Mountain, 105–107
Blair, Anthony, 176
Bogat, Marie, 164–165
Brady, Marion, 152–154
Brown, Charlie, 6, 89
Brown, Lester, 59

California earthquakes, 164–166
California education codes, 146
Camelot, 162
Carnegie Unit, 41

charter schools, 101–102
Chavez, Cesar, 126
Chico California, 144–145
Churchill, Winston, 11, 133–134
Cleveland, Harlan, 51
college requirements, 85
Colorado education, 131–132
corporate mentality, 61, 82
curriculum organization, 77

declaring war, 8
Detroit schools, 46, 101
discontinuities, 127
Disney, Walt, 163
Dorr, Rheta, 66
Duffy, Francis, 150
Duncan, Arne, 148
Duvalier, "Papa Doc," 165

education leaders, 150–151
education organizations, 15
Educational Heretics Press, 150
Eight-Year Study, 35–37
Einstein, Albert, 77, 125
Engel, Angela, 130
envisioned futures, 121
Epcot Center, 8
experiential education, 39

financial foundations, 20, 74, 147
Fiske, Edward, 1

Flushing High, 89
foreign language, 4
Fuller, Buckminster, 51

Garden Lake School, 115
Gary Indiana, 71
German atrocities, 12
global politics, 163
global populations, 58
Golden Age, 95, 158
Goodlad, John, 105

Haitian odyssey, 164
Harber, Clive, 104
hens and roosters, 26
Holmes, Edmond, 27
Holocaust survivor, 63
Holt, John, 85, 104
home economics, 79–80
horse and buggy, 21
humane politicians, 159
Hundred Years War, 12

imagineering, 8

Japan disasters, 127
Japanese atrocities, 13
Jennings, Wayne, 48
Joan of Arc, 17
Johnson, Lyndon, ix

King, Martin Luther, Jr., 126

Lawes, Lewis, 67
learning percentages, 4
Linus, 110
Little League baseball, 44
Long, Kathleen, viii

Mandela, Nelson, 19
Mead, Margaret, 1
Medford Oregon study, 44–45
Meighan, Roland, 18, 108
Middle East, 156
middle schools, 20, 137
Midway, battle of, 28
Mill, John Stuart, 141
Miller, Ron, 23
Minnesota State University, vii

misguided educators, 142
misguided politicians, 142, 148
Model Schools Project, 7
Moses, Robert, 130
MXC, 56–57

National Geographic, 154
natural disasters, 123
NCLB, 6

Ohio State University, 37, 147
one-size-fits-all, 6
organization journal editors, 94

Peanuts, 138
personalized education center, 150
personalized schools, 135
personalizing, 4
physical education, 23
pied pipers, 134
platoon system, 72
playgrounds, 26
political hot air, 168
politician visionaries, 145
Population Press, 92, 178
presidential administrations, 64
priority issues, 1
progressive education, 99
proof positive, 32

Race to the Top, 6
reaching learners, 23–24
reading via brownies, 23
research centers, 34
reward poster, 180
Russell, Bertrand, 30

Sage Report, 66
Sally (character in Peanuts), 138
San Francisco Board, 65
school dropouts, 4
Schoolboys of Barbiana, 97
Schulz, Charles, 138
Senate Investigation Committee, 157
seventh grade, 45
Sherman, Rita, 86
shop curriculum, 148–149
Shute, Chris, 136
societal conditions, 84

societal critics, 152
South Dakota, 146
startling research, 48n1–50n33

teacher education, 132
teacher unions, 12
Team of Rivals, 179
technology influences, 28
ten designs, 112–115
test score negatives, 21, 24
testing scandals, 169–171
Theobald, Robert, 121
Title III, 25
Tory Education Act, 143
traditionalist punishments, 14
traditionalists, 6
Trump, Lloyd, 94
Twenty-fourth Yearbook (NSSE), 45–46
Tyler, Ralph, 99

unifying agreement, 162
United Nations, 52

Van Til, William, 89
visionaries, 6
visionary confrontation, 14–15
visionary tables, 53

Wayne State experiment, 100
Welk music, 110
Wilson Campus School, vii, 38
win/win philosophy, 8
Wirt, William, 71
Wright brothers, 80

year-round education, 129

Zamperini, Louie, 172

About the Author

Don Glines has long been involved in the development of futures-oriented educational change with a win/win philosophy of choice. He has steadfastly stated: "If schools and universities are to be significantly better, they must be significantly different." While serving as director of the Pre-K–College Wilson Campus School, and codirector for the Center for Alternatives and Experiential Learning, Minnesota State University–Mankato, he was recognized by the *National Observer* as "the foremost apostle of educational innovation." Wilson was acknowledged as "the most innovative public school in America." It included two learner-centered education degrees without course mandates: an MS in Experiential Education, and a BS in Educational Alternatives.

His campaign to eliminate the "seventh grade," with its thirteen-year test-score range and six-year physiological spread, helped to create the original nongraded four-year middle school design. His acclaimed Lincoln Learning Laboratory was student-named the "Disneyland of South Dakota." As a futurist, he was an advisor for a lifelong learning system without schools for the proposed Minnesota Experimental City. He cofounded the National Association for Year-Round Education.

His research with the University of Oregon Medford Child Growth and Development Study proved that reaction time is an independent variable. He assisted families, staff, and school sites afflicted with chemical, food, and inhalant problems. As the first person hired by a school district—and later by a state—as a full-time consultant for innovation, he was labeled by the *Kappan* magazine as the "Vice President for Educational Heresy."

He received his BS from Springfield College, and served in the army in the Korean War. Later he studied at Occidental College and then completed his MS and PhD at the University of Oregon. His career has involved positions as a teacher, administrator, professor, planner, and consultant at elementary, secondary, university, and state department levels in both public and private sectors in four foreign countries and nine states.

The Wilson School and Don Glines Archives are housed in the Memorial Library, Minnesota State University. The Minnesota Association for Alternative Programs honored him for exemplary lifetime contributions promoting futures-oriented personalized learning choices for everyone.

ADDITIONAL WORKS BY THE AUTHOR

Balancing the School Calendar: Perspectives (chapter)
Creating Educational Futures: Continuous Mankato Wilson Alternatives
Creating Learning Communities (chapter)
Creating Humane Schools
Designing Education for the Future (chapter)
Developmental Efforts in Individualized Learning (chapter)
Educational Alternatives for Everyone
Educational Futures I: Imagining and Inventing
Educational Futures II: Options and Alternatives
Educational Futures III: Change and Reality

Educational Futures IV: Updating and Overleaping
Educational Futures V: Creating and Foresighting
Education of Elementary School Teachers (chapter)
Great Lockout in America's Citizenship Plants (with William Wirt)
Implementing Different and Better Schools
Year-Round Education Association: A History (with James Bingle)
Year-Round Education Calendar Plans
Year-Round Education: A Primer
Year-Round Education: Philosophy and History
Year-Round Education: Resources and References (with David Mussati)

. . . and over 130 articles on educational futures, change, and innovation in a wide variety of journals including: *American Secondary Education, California School Boards Journal, Changing Schools, Compact, Core Teacher, Didakometry, Education Revolution, Educational Leadership, Forum, Health Education, Illinois Teacher, Instructor Magazine, Manitoba Teacher, NASSP Bulletin, NCEA Bulletin, Paths of Learning, Pedamorphics, Personalized Education Now, Phi Delta Kappan, Teacher Magazine, Threshholds, Thrust,* and *Transescence.*

REVIEWS OF THESE PAST CONTRIBUTIONS

In *Creating Educational Futures*, trailblazer Don Glines writes that a totally new learning system is necessary and inevitable.
—Roland Meighan, *Education Now*, Nottingham, England

His *Educational Futures Trilogy* is an exemplary effort to apply the past to the future.
—Michael Marien, *Future Survey*, World Future Society, Bethesda, Maryland

Don Glines, America's most innovative educator—a vice president for heresy—describes what it takes to make all schools fabulously successful.
—Wayne Jennings, *Brain-Based Networker*, St. Paul, Minnesota

His work is a monument to human imagination and hope for the future, describing a rare lifetime opportunity to contribute to a transformation.
—Barbara Vogl, *Change Management Systems*, Soquel, California

His works represent a staggering collection . . . a goldmine of information . . . every school searching for innovative ideas should have copies.
—Robert Anderson, *Wingspan: Pedamorphosis Communiqué*, Tampa, Florida

CPSIA information can be obtained at www.ICGtesting.com
Printed in the USA
BVOW070109230112

280948BV00003B/2/P

9 781610 486637